Guide to Understanding the

Culinary Industry

Edited by Kang, Kyung Jae

(주)백산출판사

Preface & Acknowledgements

This book is the sixteenth one which I have developed since I served as a professor. When this book was first considered, my objective was to have a publication that would offer various contents, data and information related to the culinary industry which are needed to broaden our students' views on the industry. Actually I have perceived the word "culinary industry" is now being used in other countries outside Korea since 2000. Since then I had thought of producing a book connected with the culinary industry. In the consideration of the trend of culinary industry in Korea, we were at the right time to use the word "culinary industry." So I had researched and collected data and articles connected with culinary industry for 4 months. Based on these materials, In 2010 I developed the first book, 'Guide to the Culinary Industry'. This time I produced 'Guide to Understanding Culinary Industry' connected with the culinary industry.

This book has a total of 11 chapters which are Introduction to the Culinary Industry, Culinary Industry Outlook, Career Guide, Positive Attitude toward the Culinary Industry, All about Chefs, Michelin Guide: The Last Word in Gourmet Dining, Essential Culinary Terms & New Phenomena and Concepts, Commitment to Lifelong Learning, The Best Restaurants, The Great Chefs, and Korean Cuisine in the World.

In Chapter 1 Introduction to the Culinary Industry, there are four sections which are Understanding of Culinary System, Definition of Culinary Industry, Exploring Industries related to the Culinary Industry, and Analysis of Scopes among Hospitality, Culinary, Food Service, Restaurant and Catering Industry. Chapter 2 Culinary Industry Outlook consists of six sections which deal with On the Cutting Edge—Culinary Arts Careers, Culinary Industry Forecast, Restaurant Industry Trends, Consumer Trends We need to

Know by the Numbers, What's Hot for Menu Trends in 2018, and Restaurant 2025. Chapter 3 Career Guide has four sections which covers Why Study Culinary Arts? Culinary Training and Education, Job Prospects, and Building a Career in the Culinary Industry. Chapter 4 Positive Attitude toward the Culinary Industry includes four sections which are I am A Chef!, Culinary Laboratory Uniform and Code of Conduct Policy, Professionalism, and Standards of Professionalism. In Chapter 5 All about Chefs, there are nine sections and you will explore Definition of a Chef, A true Chef, The Kitchen Brigade, Difference between a Cook and a Chef, Stage, Food Preparation Workers, Culinarians, Culinary Artists, and Other Chef-related Titles. Chapter 6 Michelin Guide: The Last Word in Gourmet Dining has two sections which provide What is Michelin Guide? and The Michelin Guide Seoul. In Chapter 7 Essential Culinary Terms & New Phenomena and Concepts , there are two sections which cover Essential Culinary Terms, and New Phenomena and Concepts. In Chapter 8 Commitment to Lifelong Learning, there are four sections which introduce A Positive Attitude towards Learning, Culinary Education, Taking an Overseas Internship, and Eminent Educational Institutes. Chapter 9 The Best Restaurants has three sections which provide Michelin 3-star restaurants by Michelin Guide, The World's 50 Best Restaurants by Restaurant Magazine, and Chef's Choice Restaurants by Year. In Chapter 10 The Great Chefs, there are two sections and you will explore The Great Chefs in Culinary History, 100 Best Chefs 2018, The World's Richest Chefs in the World, and The Most Influential Chefs in the World. Chapter 11 Korean Cuisine in the World has seven sections which focus on The Role of Food or Culinary Tourism in Tourism Industry, Significance of Korean Cuisine in Tourism Industry, 5 Ways Korean Food is Symbolic of Yin and Yang Principles, The Philosophy of Korean Food, Michelin starred-Korean Restaurants in the World, Five of the Best Korean Restaurants around the World, and Promoting Korean Cuisine around the World.

I did major nothing relating to English Literature. I'm sure this book will act as an inspiration to always learn more, and encourage to gain confidence in studying English my student chefs who are eager to be successful in the culinary industry.

Eighteen years ago I was deeply impressed and shocked by the New Professional Chef

6th(ed.) which was given as a gift by one of my students, Mr. Yang, Kyu Mo. In the book there is a didactic sentence that can't be forgotten even in my dream that is "A true chef is, among other things, a lifelong student, a teacher, a craftsman, a leader, and a manager." The book has influenced tremendously and will influence me continuously. As the development of food and cuisine has never been completely one-sided, so culinary education is not one-sided. Therefore student chefs have to influence the persons engaging in culinary education, and vice versa. I want to strongly emphasize that an interaction between student chefs and the persons engaging in culinary education is of great importance in culinary education.

In writing this book I have already promised to myself more improved and updated book will be published in the next edition listing a body of information pertaining to culinary industry.

I want to thank and acknowledge the following individuals for their help and assistance in the development of this book. The persons I have recognized here are some of those nice individuals from the culinary industry who were willing to share their experiences, knowledge, and expertise.

My special thanks to: Professor Kim, Yong Mun; Professor Yi, Chae Chol Professor Choi, Bong Sun; Ex-Professor Yi, Dong Hun; Ex-Adjunct Professor Chong, Ji Yon, Hyejeon College; Mun, Sung Kwon, Chef/Owner, SamjungBonjum; Kim, Chun Hwi/Cha Un Sim, Consultant/CEO, Yoriae; Cho, Byung Sook, President, Hongsung Cooking School; Lee, Young Ju, President, Seoch'on Cooking School; Chong, Sang Yun, President, Deomat FoodSystem; Kim, Nam Dong, Owner, Deomat Kukbab; Kim, Ki Yup, Chef/Owner, Sushi Good Day; Seo Dae Hui, President, GatesKorea; Lee, Chong Hak, Chef/Owner, Obiya Restaurant; Seo, Sang Yun, General Manager, Danyang Daemyung Leisure Industry Co., ltd.; Executive Chef, Choi, Byung Uk, CJ Foodvill; Ryu, Tae Hwan, Owner/Chef, Ryunique; Jason Oh, Sous Chef, Dosa Restaurant; Chef Yi, Sang In, Sheraton Seoul D Cube City Hotel; Chef patron Um, Sung Hui, Sushishouki; Chef patron Um, Min Ho, Umgane Komtang; Chef Min, Sang Hyun, Shuchiku of 63Bldg.

I offer my thanks and gratitude to the below individuals for their help and assistance in the development of this edition.

My special thanks to: President Yi, Chae Ho, Hyejeon College; Ex-Vice President Yang, Chae Gil, FoodCulture of SAMSUNG EVERLAND INC.; M.D. Shim, Hong-Bang, Director of Hospital, VHS Medical Center; Dr. Yun, Sung Ro, Yun's Surgical Clinic; Dr. Kim, Man Gil, Gil's Dermatological Clinic; Principal Kim, Hang Sup, my close friend; Professor Cho, Nam Ji, Hyejeon College; Professor Yu, Kyong, Min, Soonnch'on University; Professor Han, Min Su, Hyejeon College; Professor Yi, Yong Hwan, Hyejeon College; Professor Song, Kyung Sook, WonKwang Health College; President Im, Kum Ran, Hwangje Food Academy; Chang, Hong Kyung, FoodCulture of SAMSUNG EVERLAND INC.; Professor Park, Ki Oh, Kyungju University; Professor Oh, Ch'ol Hwan, Korea National College of Agriculture and Fisheries.

I would like to thank my family, my wife Ko, Yon Suk, my first son, Kang, Byung Su(Bill), my only daughter, Kang, Dong Ok(Diana), and my second son, Kang, Duk(David) for their hard work, dedication, sacrifice, and assistance. Bill is working as a Senior resident at Dongshin Oriental Medicine Hospital. Diana is serving as a part-time doctor at a couple of Dental Clinics in Seoul. David is attending College of Korean Medicine, Kyung Hee University. Also I always thank for Bill, Diana, and David who are being grown up well and working very hard. Especially I want to appreciate my wife, Ko, Yon Suk, who has worked hard for our family, helping me with a precious and invaluable dedication to accomplish a better publication. As a result I complete the development of this book.

God bless you!

Kang, Kyung Jae

Professor, Department of Hotel Culinary Arts, Hyejeon College

Contents

Chapter 03 Career Guide / 55

Chapter 04 Positive Attitude toward the Culinary Industry / 73

Chapter 05 All about Chefs / 89

"Give a man a fish and he will eat for a day. Teach him how to fish and he will eat for a lifetime."

- Chinese proverb

World map indicating the Human Development Index

(based on 2015 data, published on 21 March 2017)

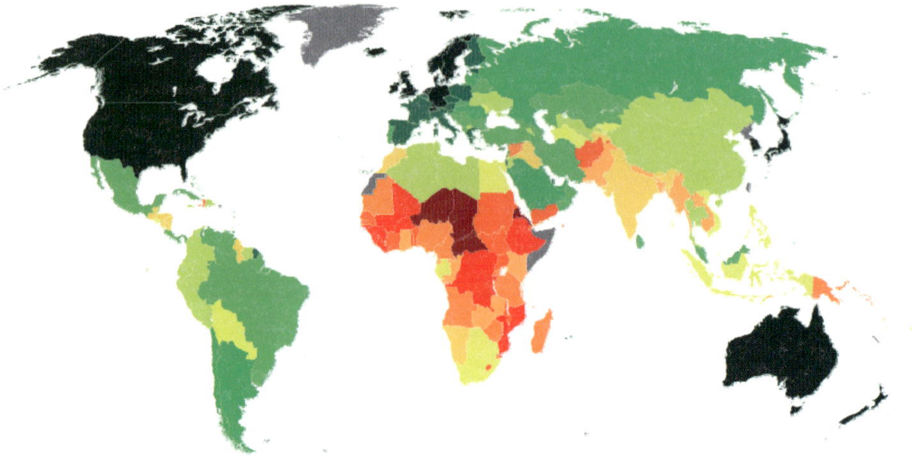

Legend

0.900+	0.650–0.699	0.400–0.449
0.850–0.899	0.600–0.649	0.350–0.399 and under
0.800–0.849	0.550–0.599	Data unavailable
0.750–0.799	0.500–0.549	
0.700–0.749	0.450–0.499	

The Human Development Index (HDI) is a composite statistic (composite index) of life expectancy, education, and per capita income indicators,

(Source : Retrieved 25 Jan 2018

https://en.wikipedia.org/wiki/Human_Development_Index)

"Education is the most powerful weapon which you can use to change the world."

- Nelson Mandela (18 July 1918 – 5 December 2013), a South African anti-apartheid revolutionary, political leader, philanthropist, and the President of South Africa from 1994 to 1999

Chapter 01

Introduction to the Culinary Industry

(Source: Retrieved 26 Jan 2018 from https://btebootcamp.com/culinary-tourism-business-or-pleasure/)

> "Food is a necessary component to life. People can live without Renoir, Mozart, Gaudi, Beckett, but they cannot live without food."
>
> - Grant Achatz (born April 25, 1974), an American chef and restaurateur often identified as one of the leaders in molecular gastronomy or progressive cuisine

1. Understanding of Culinary System

The culinary system proposed in Figure 1-1 illustrates a "Functional system of culinary arts" involving three components: Ingredients, Culinary preparations, and Culinary products. This figure describes the ingredients as the inputs, the culinary preparations as the process, and the culinary products as the outputs. The inputs are composed of meats, poultry, game, fish, shellfish, fruit, vegetable, fresh herb, dairy, egg, dry goods, etc. The process involves arts of chefs, skills of chefs, culinary activities of chefs, cooking equipment, and kitchen. The outputs consist of Korean cuisine, Western cuisine, Chinese cuisine, Japanese cuisine, ethnic cuisine, innovative cuisine, etc. This culinary System provides a way to understand how chefs perform their tasks and duties, and how to maximize their performance.

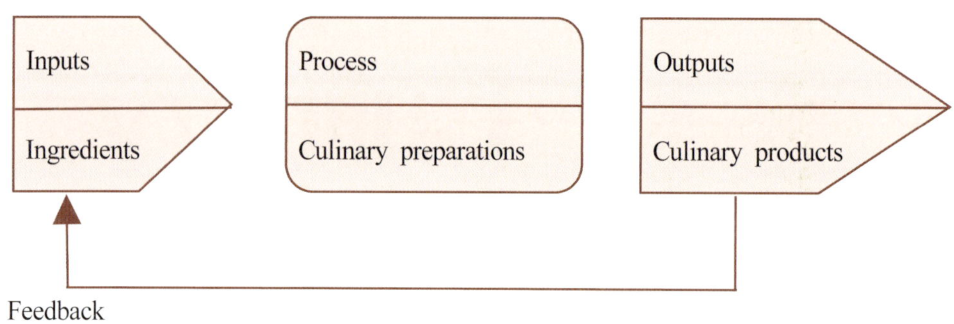

[Figure 1-1] A systematic approach to Culinary arts

2. Definition of Culinary Industry

In the narrow back streets of Hong Kong, you can perch on a stool in a modest stall, and slurp down a bowl of piping hot prawn wonton noodle soup for a few dollars. This bustling little eatery is the smallest of small businesses. But it's part of a vast global industry (Murray, 2007).

When we are discussing about culinary industry, our first task is to know the meanings of culinary, arts, and culinary arts. To look up definitions of the term "culinary" is based upon six dictionaries on the internet. Table 1-1 shows us that the term "culinary" means something connected with cooking (which means the activity of preparing food and food itself), cookery (which means the art or practice of preparing food and kitchen), kitchen and food, that is to say the culinary has four meanings such as the activity of preparing food, the art or practice of preparing food, kitchen and food itself, (Education.yahoo, Encarta.msn, Merriam-webster, Dictionary.cambridge, En.wiktionary, Whatscookingamerica, n.d.).

A dictionary definition of the term "art" is skill that is attained by study, practice, or observation (Education.yahoo, n.d.), but generally it is defined as the ability or skill involved in doing or making something (Answers, n.d.). Therefore, the term "culinary arts" is defined as all about the art of cooking, as all about being concerned with the way food is prepared and served, and as all about making things easier and all functions more efficient in the kitchens.

On the other hand, the term "industry" is generally used to describe any grouping of businesses that share a common method of generating profits, such as the "movie industry", the "automobile industry", or the "cattle industry" It is also used specifically to refer to an area of economic production focused on manufacturing which involves large amounts of upfront capital investment before any profit can be realized, also called "heavy industry" (Info.abaara, n.d.).

When we say "food", drinking beverages is an implied and associated activity. Accordingly as the term "culinary industry" is defined below, food is used along with beverages.

Hence the term "culinary industry" is defined as organized economic activities connected with the production and provision of food and beverages that are not prepared in the home, and other related economic activities based on food and beverages and kitchens. In foreign countries the word "culinary industry" seen on the homepages of many culinary schools, colleges and universities, in many articles of journals related to culinary industry, and so on, is too numerous to be counted (Culinaryprograms, n.d.; Jwu, 2008; Acfchefs, n.d.; Zahari, et al., 2009; Johnson, 2009). But in Korea the word "culinary industry" cannot be seen on the homepages of many culinary schools, colleges and universities, and in many articles of journals related to culinary arts, and so on.

▌Table 1-1▌ Meanings of Culinary

<table>
<tr><th rowspan="2">Meaning
Source</th><th colspan="2">Cooking</th><th colspan="2">Cookery</th><th rowspan="2">Kitchen</th><th rowspan="2">Food</th></tr>
<tr><th>Activity</th><th>Food</th><th>Art</th><th>Kitchen</th></tr>
<tr><td rowspan="2">① American Heritage Dictionary of the English Language</td><td rowspan="2"></td><td rowspan="2"></td><td>The art or practice of preparing food</td><td>A place for cooking</td><td rowspan="2">Of or relating to a kitchen</td><td rowspan="2"></td></tr>
<tr><td colspan="2">Of or relating to cookery</td></tr>
<tr><td rowspan="2">② Encarta® World English Dictionary, North American Edition</td><td>The process or activity of preparing food for eating</td><td>Food that has been prepared for eating
Ex.)
She doesn't like my cooking.</td><td rowspan="2"></td><td rowspan="2"></td><td rowspan="2"></td><td rowspan="2">relating to food</td></tr>
<tr><td colspan="2">relating to cooking</td></tr>
<tr><td rowspan="2">③ Merriam-Webster's Online Dictionary, 11th Edition</td><td rowspan="2"></td><td rowspan="2"></td><td>The art or practice of cooking</td><td>An establishment for cooking</td><td rowspan="2">of or relating to the kitchen</td><td rowspan="2"></td></tr>
<tr><td colspan="2">of or relating to cookery</td></tr>
<tr><td rowspan="2">④ Cambridge International Dictionary of English</td><td>Preparing or cooking food</td><td>Ex.)
I love my dad's cooking (=the food that he cooks).</td><td rowspan="2"></td><td rowspan="2"></td><td rowspan="2">connected withkitchens</td><td rowspan="2"></td></tr>
<tr><td colspan="2">connected with cooking</td></tr>
<tr><td>⑤ Wiktionary</td><td colspan="2">Relating to the activity of cooking</td><td colspan="2">Relating to the practice of cookery</td><td>Of, or relating to a kitchen</td><td></td></tr>
<tr><td>㉖ Linda's Culinary Dictionary</td><td colspan="2">anything to do with cooking</td><td></td><td></td><td></td><td></td></tr>
</table>

Remark : When the word "culinary" was entered in "the Word or phrase Box" and clicked the "Search" button in OneLook Dictionary Search (http://www.onelook.com/), the author referenced the first 5 dictionaries and the last one connected with culinary field.

(Source : Kang, Kyung Jae, Guide to the Culinary Industry, 2010: 20)

3. Exploring Industries related to the Culinary Industry

Various definitions on restaurant industry, catering industry, hospitality industry and food service industry are explored. These definitions explored form the basis for the comparison among scopes of each industry. Let's explore these industries in more detail.

1) Food Service Industry

The food service industry encompasses all of the activities, services, and business functions involved in preparing and serving food to people eating away from home. This includes all types of restaurants from fine dining to fast food. It also includes institutional food operations at locations such as schools and hospitals, as well as other specialty vendors such as food truck operators and catering businesses (Moore, n.d.).

Foodservice and food service appear to be interchangeable with only a difference in spelling, although it has been suggested that in the USA, the two words were combined to help avoid any confusion and emphasize the fact that the term involves more than the service of food (Journal compilation, 2009).

In the UK, the term catering is used to embrace the industry; hence, catering industry is the term used to cover all aspects of the foodservice (USA) industry. More recently in the UK, the use of the term food service has become popular and often used synonymously with catering. Hence, a hospital catering officer is responsible for the food service. In the USA, on the other hand, catering tends to refer more to the physical provision of food by a caterer or at a catered event

(Ibid.). Accordingly, the former is chosen by the author for consistency and unity of terms used in this text.

There is the other way to define and classify the foodservice industry, with many textbooks also dividing the industry into two broad segments or categories: The commercial (profit) sector and the public (cost sector, subsidized or welfare) sector. Notwithstanding, it is fair to say that the foodservice industry is international, highly diverse and includes a range of outlets that serve food and beverages, perhaps for payment, to people who want them, but this may or may not be the primary goal of the business (Ibid., 3). Figure 1-2 shows us the diversity of the industry.

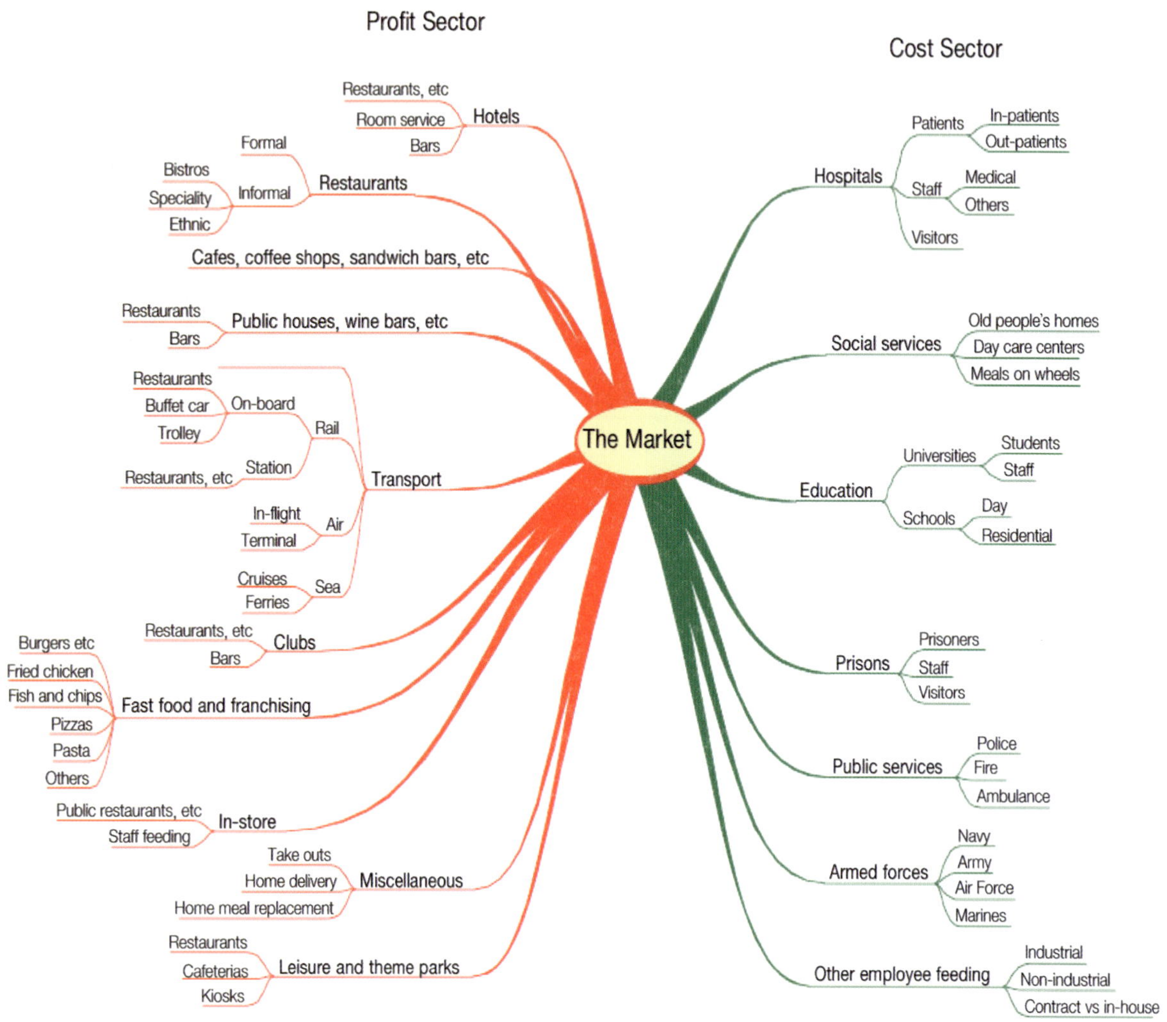

[Figure 1–2] The diversity of the foodservice industry
(Source : Journal compilation, 2009: 3)

2) Restaurant Industry

NRA defines restaurant industry as all meals/snacks prepared away from home, including all takeout meals and beverages (Riehle, 2008). Restaurant industry has four general segments according to the service customers receive: full service, quick service, eating and drinking place and retail host (Akers, n.d.).

3) Catering Industry

Generally, catering is defined as the act of providing food and drink for an event, and as the department responsible for providing such services (travel service dictionary). On the other hand, North American Industry Classification System (NAICS) codes this catering industry with a number, 722320. This industry comprises establishments primarily engaged in providing single event-based food services. These establishments generally have equipment and vehicles to transport meals and snacks to events and/or prepare food at an off-premise site. Banquet halls with catering staff are included in this industry. Examples of events catered by establishments in this industry are graduation parties, wedding receptions, business or retirement luncheons, and trade shows (NAICS, 2017).

4) Hospitality Industry

As stated by DeShields, the hospitality industry is defined as the activity of providing lodging, food and beverage, and recreational services, which include but are not limited to hotels, motels, clubs, casinos, restaurants, recreation facilities, tourism, cruise lines, and theme parks (DeShields, n.d.).

As stated in a research by PPRC (The Pacific Northwest Pollution Prevention

Resource Center), thc hospitality industry covers a wide ranging number of services and activities. It includes travel related services such as lodging, restaurants, food services and convention centers. Also included are entertainment services including golf courses, sports arenas, amusement parks, movie theaters, playhouses, concert venues, tour services, and national and state parks, to name but a few (PPRC, 1998).

In a report on the economic impact of San Antonio's hospitality industry, Butler and Stefl used the lines of business defined by the North American Industrial Classification System to define the scope of hospitality industry in of San Antonio.Table 1-2 shows that hospitality industry is separated into 4 subsectors such as lodging subsector, restaurants and catering subsector, transportation and travel subsector, and entertainment subsector based on the North American Industrial Classification System (Butler and Stefl, 2008).

Table 1-2 NAICS Codes For The Hospitality Industry

Lodging	7211 Hotels, motels, etc. 7212 RV parks and recreational camps
Restaurants and Catering	7221 Full service restaurants 7222 Limited-service eating places 7223 Special food services 7224 Drinking places
Transportation and Travel	48111 Scheduled air transportation 48521 Interurban and rural bus transportation 48551 Charter buses 48599 Other ground passenger transportation 48711 Scenic and sightseeing transportation 48811 Airport operations 53211 Passenger car rental and leasing

	56152 Tour operators 56159 Other travel arrangement services 81293 Parking lots and garages
Entertainment	51213 Motion picture exhibition 7111 Performing arts companies 71121 Spectator sports 7113 Promoters of performing arts 7115 Independent artists, writers and performers 7121 Museums, historical sites, zoos, etc. 71311 Amusement and theme parks 71312 Amusement arcades 71391 Golf courses and country clubs 71399 Other amusement and recreation

(Source : Butler, Richard V. and Mary E. Stefl, 2008, "The ECONOMIC IMPACT of San Antonio's HOSPITALITY INDUSTRY," San Antonio Area Tourism Council, Retrieved Jan. 16, 2010 from http://www.sariverfoundation.org/downloads/visitor_study.pdf/benchmark/2009/html/naicsdef.html)

4. Analysis of Scopes among Hospitality, Culinary, Food Service, Restaurant and Catering Industry

As stated by Armstrong and others, food service and culinary industry come under the umbrella of hospitality services (Armstrong, Callie, et al., 2006). Thus it's no doubt that culinary industry, food service industry, restaurant industry, and catering industry belong to hospitality industry.

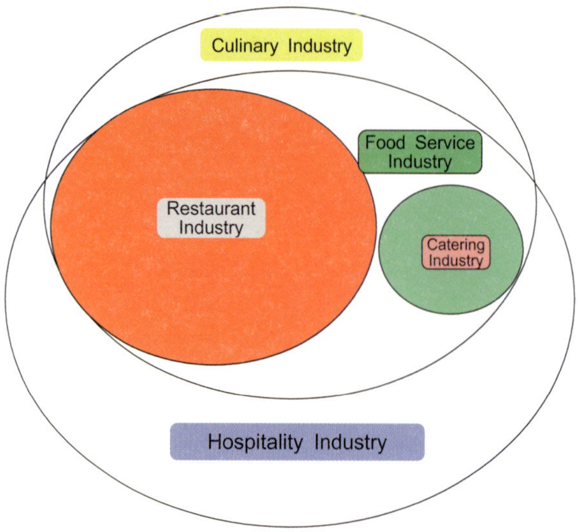

[Figure 1–3] Comparing scopes among hospitality industry, culinary industry, food service industry, restaurant industry, and catering industry

(Source : Kang, Kyung Jae, Guide to the Culinary Industry, 2010: 31)

Based upon the definitions on food service industry, restaurant industry, catering industry, and hospitality industry explored, the food service industry can be literally defined as an industry that provides food and beverages outside the home. Restaurant industry can be defined an industry related to a place where food and beverages are sold and served to customers. Catering industry is an industry related to the business of providing food and drink for an event at a remote site. Restaurant industry doesn't include catering industry. Restaurant industry is one thing, and catering industry is another.

Food service industry and restaurant industry are similar in that both industries prepare and serve food and beverages. But food service industry is different fromrestaurant industry in that food service industry include establishments primarily engaged in selling snack and nonalcoholic beverage and other related products (e.g., coffee beans, mugs, coffee makers), which restaurant industry excludes, and in that food service industry comprises establishments primarily engaged in providing one of the following food services: (1) at the customers' location (food service contractors); (2) a location designated by the customer (caterers); or (3) from motorized vehicles or nonmotorized carts (mobile food services), which restaurant industry excludes. Thus restaurant industry comes under the umbrella of food service industry.

On the other hand, Section 2 in Chapter 1 shows the term "culinary industry" is defined as organized economic activities connected with the production and provision of food and beverages that are not prepared in the home, and other related organized economic activities based on food, beverages and kitchens.

In that both culinary industry and food service industry prepare and serve food and beverages, both industries are similar. But culinary industry is different from food service industry in that culinary industry includes other related economic activities based on food, beverages and kitchens, which food service industry excludes. In terms of related economic activities based on food, beverages and kitchens, people in culinary industry enter into wider areas than those in food service industry. In addition, there are more career opportunities in culinary industry than in food service industry because people in culinary industry possess more culinary skills than those in restaurant industry.

To conclude, restaurant industry doesn't include catering industry. Restaurant industry is one thing, and catering industry is another. Catering industry comes under the umbrella of food service industry, restaurant industry under the umbrella of food service industry, and again food service industry under the umbrella of culinary industry. Culinary industry, food service industry, restaurant industry, and catering industry come under the umbrella of hospitality industry, which includes culinary industry with the exception of those job opportunities. Figure 1-3 shows comparing scopes among hospitality industry, culinary industry, food service industry, restaurant industry, and catering industry.

Note

- ethnic : connected with or relating to different racial or cultural groups of people
- perch : (usually foll by on) to alight, rest, or cause to rest on or as if on a perch
- stool : a simple seat without a back or arms
- stall : a small area of a room that is separated from the main part of the room by walls or curtains
- slurp down : to eat noisily
- piping : (used of heat) extremely
- bustling : full of energetic and noisy activity
- eatery : a restaurant
- upfront : frank and honest
- capital : money and possessions, especially a large amount of money used for producing more wealth or for starting a new business
- journal : a serious magazine or newspaper which is published regularly, usually about a specialist subject
- lodging : a temporary place to stay
- arena : a large flat area surrounded by seats used for sports or entertainment
- playhouse : a theatre. This is now only used in the names of theatres.
- venue : the place where a public event or meeting happens
- to name but a few : 몇 가지만 말하자면
- account for sth : to form the total of something

References

AAA, 2017, "Foodie Travelers Are Embracing the Culinary Travel Trend," Retrieved Jan. 16, 2018 from http://newsroom.aaa.com/2017/04/foodie-travelers-embracing-culinary-travel-trend/

Akers, Helen, (NA). Major Segments of the Restaurant Industry. Retrieved Dec. 26, 2017 from http://smallbusiness.chron.com/major-segments-restaurant-industry-25986.html

Butler, Richard V. and Mary E. Stefl, 2008, "The ECONOMIC IMPACT of San Antonio's HOSPITALITY INDUSTRY," San Antonio Area Tourism Council, Retrieved Jan. 16, 2010 from http://www.sariverfoundation.org/downloads/visitor_study.pdf/benchmark/2009/html/naicsdef.html

Culinaryprograms, "A History of Le Cordon Bleu," Retrieved Dec. 27, 2009 from http://www.culinaryprograms.com/cordon.htm

DeShields, Gregory L., "Choosing a Career in the Hospitality Industry," Retrieved Dec. 26, 2009 from http://hotel-industry.learnhub.com/lesson/13362-choosing-a-career-in-the-hospitality-industry

Info.abaara, "Industry," Retrieved Jan. 5, 2010 from http://info.abaara.com/pac/Industry

Johnson, Erik, 2009, "Deciding to Start a New Career in the Culinary Arts," Dec. 18, Retrieved Jan. 9, 2010 from http://www.goarticles.com/cgi-bin/showa.cgi?C=2392818

Journal compilation 2009, Wiley Periodicals, Inc, Journal of Foodservice, 20, pp.1-3

Kang, Kyung Jae, Guide to the Culinary Industry, 2010: 20

Moore, Allison, Retrieved Dec. 26, 2017 from http://study.com/academy/lesson/food-service-industry-definition-history.html

Murray, Sarah, Nov 15, 2007, "The World's Biggest Industry," Retrieved Dec. 26, 2017 from https://www.forbes.com/2007/11/11/growth-agriculture-business-forbeslife-food07-cx_sm_1113bigfood.html#21bd603a373e

PPRC, 1998, "Pollution Prevention in the Hospitality Sector," August, Retrieved Dec. 26, 2009 from http://www.pprc.org/pubs/hosptlty.cfm

Riehle, Hudson, 2008, "Restaurant Industry 2008 and Beyond," Rhode Island Hospitality & Tourism Association Economic Outlook Breakfast, Oct. 21, Retrieved Jan. 5, 2010 from www.rihospitality.org/pdf/Hudson Riehle.ppt,

Zahari, Mohd Salehuddin Mohd, et al., 2009, "Gastronomy: An Opportunity for Malaysian Culinary Educators," InternationalEducation Studies, May, 2(2), Retrieved Dec. 26, 2009 from http://ccsenet.org/journal/index.php/ies/article/view/1687/1632

Retrieved Jan. 3, 2018 from http://www.travel-industry-dictionary.com/catering.html

Retrieved Jan. 13, 2018 from http://encarta.msn.com/encnet/features/dictionary/

Retrieved Jan. 14, 2018 from http://en.wikipedia.org/wiki/

Retrieved Jan. 14, 2018 from http://www.answers.com/topic/craft

Retrieved Jan. 14, 2018 from http://education.yahoo.com/,

Retrieved Jan. 14, 2018 from http://www.merriam-webster.com/,

Retrieved Jan. 14, 2018 from http://en.wiktionary.org/,

Retrieved Jan. 14, 2018 from http://whatscookingamerica.net/

Retrieved Jan. 14, 2018 from www.acfchefs.org

Retrieved Jan. 29, 2010 from http://outfood.wu.ac.kr/

Retrieved Jan. 29, 2010 from http://uni.shoseo.ac.kr/department/food1.asp.

Retrieved Jan. 9, 2018 from https://www.census.gov/cgi-bin/sssd/naics/naicsrch?code=722320 &search=2017 NAICS Search

Retrieved Jan. 29, 2010 from http://portal.sjcu.ac.kr/jsp/subject/new_subject.jsp?p_showmenu =3&s_showmenu=3&p_ifrmurl=/jsp/subject/guide/new_hotel_guide06.jsp

Retrieved Jan. 9, 2018 from https://en.wikipedia.org/wiki/Culinary_tourism#/media/File:Terrace_ cafe,_Rue_de_Buci,_Paris_July_2010.jpg

Chapter 02

Culinary Industry Outlook

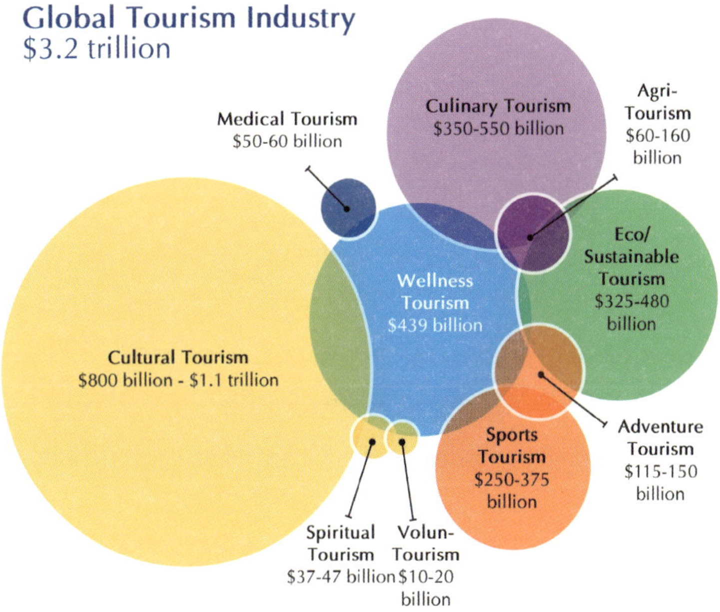

(Source : Retrieved 24 Jan 2018 https://en.wikipedia.org/wiki/Culinary_tourism#/media/)

"If you're happy, you eat. If you're sad, you eat. You lose a job, you eat. You get a job, you eat. It's, you know, it's addiction."

- Barbara Cook (October 25, 1927 – August 8, 2017), an American singer and actress

As stated in Section 4 in Chapter 1, Foodservice industry comes under the umbrella of culinary industry, and agin restaurant industry comes under the umbrella of food service industry. Since there is no culinary industry statistics. restaurant industry statistics is used instead in Chapter 2.

1. On the Cutting Edge - Culinary Arts Careers

1) The Reality

Those in culinary arts generally work long hours. The work is very physically demanding—many hours of standing, heavy lifting, mixing large vats of food, and rolling out many pounds of dough. The unusual hours, which include weekends, evenings, and holidays, do not allow for much of a social life. In spite of these negative aspects of the field, there is high level of satisfaction reported by those working in it. The Princeton Review Guide to Your Career quotes one professional chef: "(this field) is only for the very crazy. It is hard work, it is gruelling work, it is important work, and still, I would do nothing else."

2) The Career Path

The career path for those trained in the culinary arts has become less clear-cut in recent years. In the past, one moved from preparation chef to assistant chef to head chef. The large number of training programs available have caused the field to become more competitive and only those with exceptional skills become head chef.

Specialization is also important for those who want to move up.

According to The Occupational Outlook Handbook, Chefs and cooks are responsible for preparing meals that are pleasing to the palate and the eye. Chefs are the most highly skilled and trained of all kitchen workers. Although the terms chef and cook are still used interchangeably, cooks are less skilled.

A chef with extensive experience may be promoted to executive chef, a part of the managerial team running a dining establishment. Other members of this team include the general manager and assistant managers. Occasionally, in smaller establishments, the executive chef serves as the general manager. The executive chef is responsible for running the kitchen, and his or her duties include selecting menu items and analyzing the recipes of the dishes to determine food, labor, overhead costs and to assign prices to the various dishes.

3) Earnings

Earnings vary geographically and by type of establishment. The Occupational Outlook Handbook reports that the median annual wage of chefs and head cooks was $47,390 in May 2016 (Occupational Employment Statistics, 2016). How much does a Executive Chef make? Executive chefs for hotels earn the most, on average. The median annual Executive Chef salary is $63,874, as of January 02, 2018, with a range usually between $54,414～$77,322, however this can vary widely depending on a variety of factors (See, Figure 2-1; salary.com, 2017). Earnings of cooks, chefs, and other kitchen workers are considerably lower.

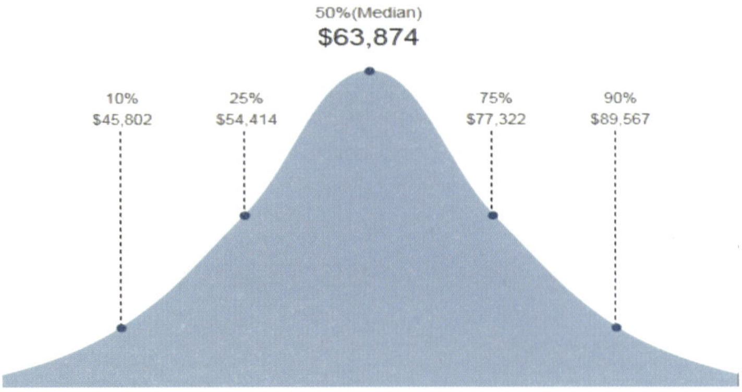

[Figure 2-1] The median annual Executive Chef salary
(Source: Retrieved Jan. 16, 2018 from https://www1.salary.com/Executive-Chef-Salary.html)

4) The Outlook

According to national data from the Bureau of Labor Statistics, the bureau's Employment Projections program anticipates about 15 percent growth through 2025 in the number of Americans working in restaurant kitchens; nearly 200,000 more line cooks and chefs will be needed (Moskin, 2015). Job openings for chefs, cooks, and other kitchen workers are expected to be plentiful through the year 2025. Much of this job growth will result from a high rate of turnover. An increase in restaurant industry sales will contribute to this growth (See Figure 2-2; WorkBC, 2018).

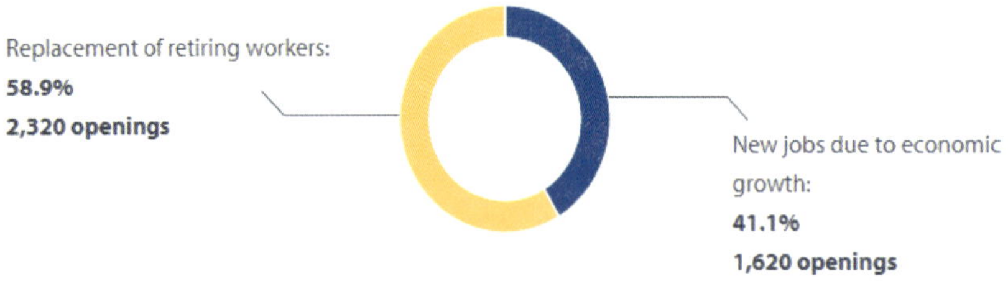

[Figure 2-2] Composition of Job openings
(Source: Retrieved Jan. 16, 2010 from https://www.workbc.ca/careers/6321#bc-labour-market-outlook)

Note

- On the Cutting Edge : (for someone) to be trendy and very up-to-date; (for something) to be of the latest design
- avocation : a hobby or minor occupation
- vat : a large tank or tub used to hold liquid, especially in industry
- gruelling : extremely tiring and difficult, and demanding great effort and determination

2. Culinary Industry Forecast

1) Booming industry

In February 2017, Hospitality News by the CRA(Colorado Restaurant Association) delivers that the restaurant industry is the nation's second-largest private sector employer with more than 14.5 million people employed in more than 1 million locations (Colorado Restaurant Association, 2017). Furthermore, Bureau of Labor Statistics suggests that the culinary industry will experience one of the largest increases in new jobs until 2026. Employment of chefs and head cooks is projected to grow 10 percent from 2016 to 2026, faster than the average for all occupations. Most job opportunities for chefs and head cooks are expected to be in food services, including restaurants. Job opportunities will result from the need to replace workers who leave the occupation (BLS, 2017).

However, competition should be keen for jobs in the top kitchens of higher end restaurants. Although job growth will create many new positions, the overwhelming majority of job openings will stem from the need to replace workers who leave this large occupational group. Many chef, cook, and food preparation worker jobs are attractive to people seeking first-time or short-term employment, additional income, or a flexible work schedule. Employers typically hire a large number of part-time workers, but many of these workers soon transfer to other occupations or stop working, creating numerous openings for those entering the field. At higher end restaurants, the fast pace, long hours, and high energy levels required to succeed also cause some top chefs and cooks to leave for other jobs, creating job openings (Ctculinary, n.d.; Livecareer, 2009).

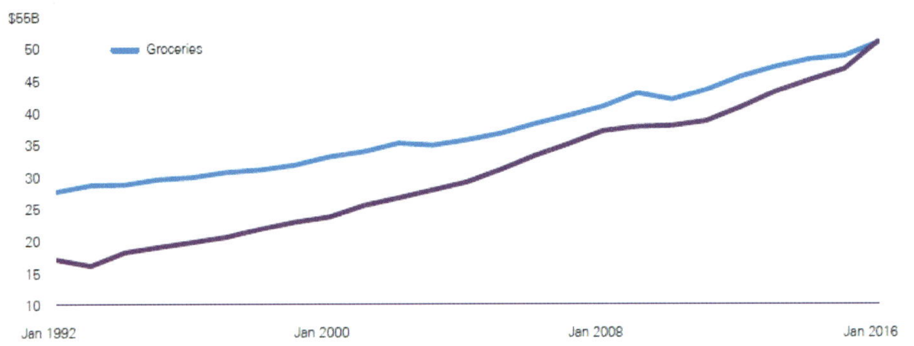

[Figure 2-3] Dining out growing at expense of eating in
(Source: Michelle Jamrisko, "Americans' Spending on Dining Out Just Overtook Grocery Sales for the First Time Ever," Retrieved Jan. 16, 2010 from https://www.bloomberg.com/news/articles/2015-04-14/americans-spending-on-dining-out-just-overtook-grocery-sales-for-the-first-time-ever)

2) Lucrative industry

In 2015, Bloomberg reports that spending on food away from home overtook spending on groceries for the first time in history (See Figure 2-3; Bloomberg Markets, 2015). In February 2017, Hospitality News by the CRA(Colorado

Restaurant Association) says that total U.S. foodservice industry sales will exceed $790 billion, 4% of GDP, and U.S. consumers will spend approximately $2.2 billion per day on food away from home (Colorado Restaurant Association, 2017). Especially, four out of five consumers agree that going out to a restaurant is a better way to use their leisure time than cooking and cleaning up. The dollar signs prove it (Tellefsen, n.d.). Let's look at the following analysis (See Table 2-1; 2-2; Figure 2-4; 1-4; 1-5).

[Figure 2-4] Restaurant Industry's Share of the Food Dollar
(Source: NRA, Restaurant Industry 2017 and Beyond, May 20, 2017)

Table 2-1 2017 Restaurant Industry Overview Projected

Annual Sales	$799 billion/ $766 billion (2016)
Annual F&B Purchases	$284 billion
Locations	More than 1 million
Employees	14.7 million
Restaurant-Industry Share of the Food Dollar	48%
Tableservice Restaurant Sales	$263 billion/ $254 billion (2016)
Limited-service Restaurant Sales	$234 billion/ $222 billion (2016)
Snack and Nonalcoholic Beverage Bar Sales	$40.8 billion/ $38.4 billion (2016)

(Source: NRA, "Restaurant Industry 2017 and Beyond," May 20, 2017, Retrieved Jan. 2, 2018 fromhttps://www.restaurant.org/Downloads/PDFs/Events-Groups/Fast-Casual-Show-State-of-Industry-Presentation-Ma.pdf)

Table 2-2 2017 Restaurant Industry Sales Projection: $798.7 Billion

Type of Establishment	2017 Estimated Sales
Commercial restaurant services	$736.3
Eating places	$551.7
Bars and Taverns(Drinking places)	$19.8
Managed services	$53.6
Lodging places	$36.1
Retail, vending, recreation, mobile	$75.2
Noncommercial restaurant services	$59.7
Military restaurant services	$2.7

(Source: NRA, "2017 Restaurant Industry POCKET FACTBOOK," Retrieved Jan. 2, 2018 from https://www.restaurant.org/Downloads/PDFs/News-Research/Pocket_Factbook_FEB_2017-FINAL.pdf)

Conducted by the University of Colorado Boulder's Leeds School of Business, the economic-impact analysis found that the restaurateurs self-reported spending $3.7 million from more than 100 Colorado producers in 2014 on items such as bread, meat and dairy products. That translated to a $7.4 million direct and indirect impact with the money staying with local companies and farmers who then could pump it back into their business (Sealover, 2015).

On the other hand, a report on the economic impact of San Antonio's hospitality industry shows that among lodging subsector, restaurants and catering subsector, transportation and travel subsector, and entertainment subsector of hospitality industry, the restaurants and catering subsector made the largest contribution to the local economy, accounting for 42.2% of the total economic impact, or $4.6 billion. The vast majority of this large impact was due to full-service or limited-service restaurants and eating places ($1.9 billion and $2.2 billion respectively), with the remainder coming from catering services and drinking establishments (See Figure 2-5; Butler and Stefl, 2008).

In conclusion, we can see restaurants and catering subsector plays a key role in the overall economic impact on a city or country. So the culinary industry is an exciting and dynamic field, offering a number of opportunities for those who have a passion for cooking and strong creative skills. Let's get into the world of culinary industry.

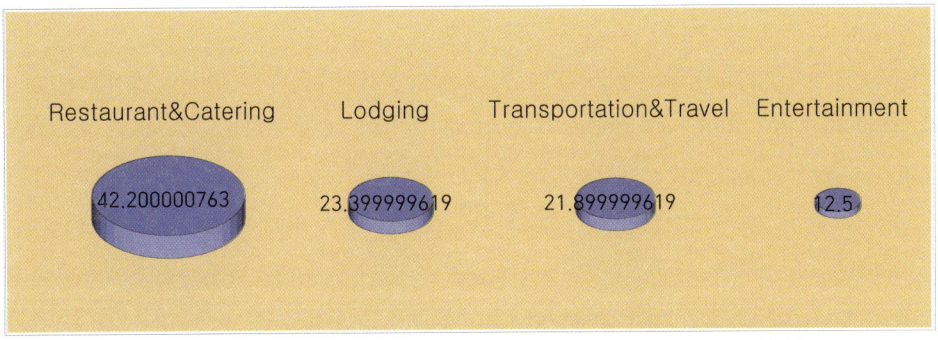

[Figure 2-5] The Economic Impact of the Hospitality Industry in 2008

(Source : Butler, Richard V. and Mary E. Stefl, 2008, "The ECONOMIC IMPACT of San Antonio's HOSPITALITY INDUSTRY," San Antonio Area Tourism Council, Retrieved Jan. 16, 2010 from http://www.sariverfoundation.org/downloads/visitor_study.pdf/benchmark/2009/html/naicsdef.html)

3. Restaurant Industry Trends

These seven key trends are driving innovation in the restaurant industry, and theyshould be also at the heart of a chef and an innovation strategy (QSR; Franchise Help; Nerac; PR Newswire, Ibid., KPMG, 2016).

1) Preferences for healthier food options

① Consumers prefer to eat at home and, if dining out, are inclined to consume healthier and less processed foods.

② Restaurants have been making attempts to influence consumption patterns by deploying attractive pricing and marketing techniques.

2) Modification of menu items driven by regulatory norms

① With nutrition labeling requirements being enforced by the Affordable Care Act, restaurant operators are obligated to make changes to menus to show the calorie counts of their products.

② Restaurant chains are focusing on narrower and more specialized menus with an objective to enhance quality standards, speed, and service.

3) Increase in food service options

① Restaurants have been losing market share to supermarkets, which have started stocking wide ranges of ready-to-eat meals; further, an increasing number of them have added eat-in areas.

② Additionally, an increase in the number of players offering similar products clustered in the same location is leading to saturation—resulting in fewer unique consumers per outlet.

4) Technological advancements

① Restaurant chains are adopting new technologies for ordering, payment, and loyalty programs to offer convenient and intuitive applications for customers.

② Analysts foresee creative uses for Google Glass, such as glass-wearing servers using face recognition technology to quickly locate patrons in crowded bars. Data from Apple Pay and other electronic wallet solutions will also make it easier to personalize customer experience.

5) Environment sustainability

① Restaurants have been focusing on reducing food waste to manage rising costs and to "go green."

② Rising awareness of sustainability, especially among millennials, is forcing restaurants to implement environment-friendly and sustainable practices.

6) Focus on Generation Z

① Restaurants are currently trying to appeal to millennials and are competing for the attention of this social media-savvy generation. They also need to be mindful of Generation Z as younger teens are beginning to make their own decisions aboutwhere to eat and what to eat.

② This demographic would also demand high-tech service, louder music, moving visuals to get heightened experiences. Restaurants will have to adapt and modify their operating strategy to attract this target segment.

7) Inclination towards global cuisines

① Increase in preferences for global/ethnic cuisines is prompting restaurants to diversify their businesses.

② According to a survey by the NRA, 80 percent of consumers eat at least one ethnic cuisine per month.

4. Consumer Trends We need to Know by the Numbers

There is no denying the fact that the globe continues to urbanize. Single people areon the rise. The people on the planet are also getting older and are more interested in health and wellness. And if you are paying for stuff with cash—not a card—you are now in the minority. The National Restaurant Association surveyed nearly 1,300 professional chefs—members of the American Culinary Federation—on which food, cuisines, beverages and culinary themes will be hot trends on restaurant menus in 2017 (NRA, 2017).

- 40%: Consumers who say diet-specific food options would make them choose one restaurant over another.
- 54%: Consumers who say they would order breakfast items more often if restaurants offered them all day.

- 63%: Millennials who eat a wider variety of ethnic cuisines now than they did two years ago.
- 49%: Consumers who would buy meal kits to prepare at home if their favorite restaurant offered them.
- 56%: Consumers who say their primary reason for preferring locally sourced food is that it supports farms and producers in their communities.
- 60%: Consumers who say availability of environmentally friendly food would make them choose one restaurant over another.
- 80%: Millennials who have used free Wi-Fi in a restaurant in the last year.
- 20%: Consumers who say they would rather use technology than interact with restaurant staff.
- 30%: Consumers who say technology makes them dine out or order takeout or delivery more often.
- 42%: Consumers who say the ability to order online would make them choose one restaurant over another.
- 45%: Consumers who say technology makes restaurant visits and ordering more complicated.
- 34%: Smartphone users who have used their phone to pay for a restaurant meal.

Note

- keen : extreme or very strong
- stem from sth : to start or develop as the result of something
- lucrative : (especially of a business, job or activity) producing a lot of money
- overtake : to go past something by being a greater amount or degree
- translate : to cause a particular situation or result
- Affordable Care Act : 오바마케어(환자보호 및 부담적정보험법; ObamaCare, Patient Protection and Affordable Care Act), 버락 오바마 대통령이 주도하는 미국의 의료보험 시스템 개혁 법안으로 정식 명칭은 '환자보호 및 부담적정보험법(Patient Protection and Affordable Care Act)'이다. 흔히 ACA란 약칭으로 쓰인다. 민영보험에만 의존하는 의료보험 시스템을 바꾸고, 미국 전국민에게 2014년까지 건강보험 가입을 의무화하는 것이 핵심으로 오바마 대통령이 8년 재임 기간 중 최대 업적으로 꼽고 있는 것이다(한경 경제용어사전, 한국경제신문/한경닷컴).
- intuitive : based on feelings rather than facts or proof
- millennials : 1980년대에서 2000년대 사이에 태어난 세대.
- Generation Z : Z세대는 1995년 이후 태어난 19세 미만의 청소년을 뜻한다. 1990년대 중반 탄생한 X세대와 2000년대 초반 새로운 밀레니엄(Y2000)을 이끌 주역으로 부상한 Y세대를 잇고 있다.
- savvy : knowing a lot about something and able to make good judgments about it
- mindful : careful about or conscious of something

5. What's Hot for Menu Trends in 2018

The National Restaurant Association releases its annual survey of 700 professional chefs—members of the American Culinary Federation—to predict food and beverage trends at restaurants in 2018. The annual "What's Hot" list gives a peek into which food, beverages and culinary concepts will be the new items on restaurant menus that everyone is talking about in 2018 (NRA. 2017).

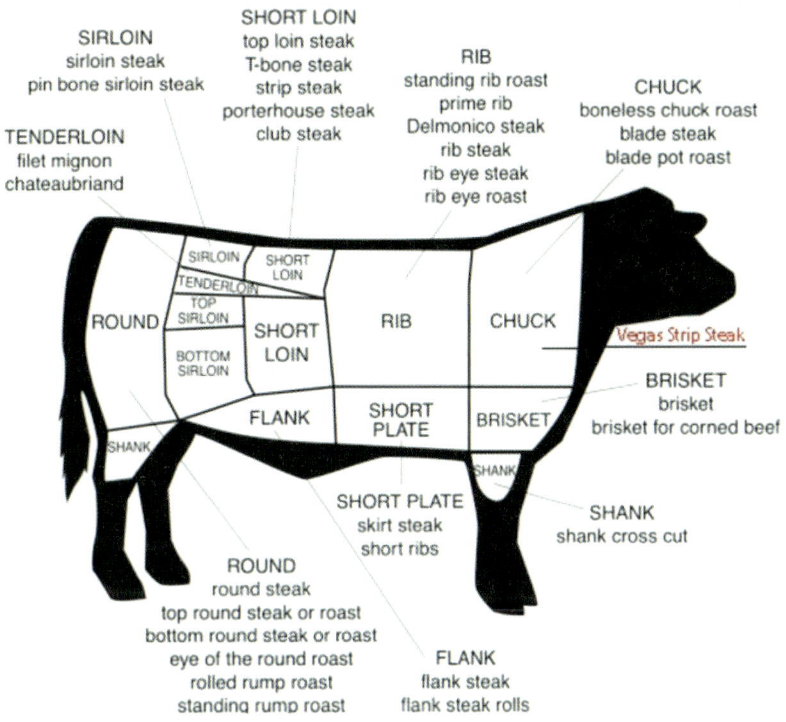

[Figure 2–6] The location of Vegas Strip Steak

Description : Chuck no more: A new cut of steak, the 'Vegas Strip', has been discovered hiding in an area of the cow that is normally used for chuck.

(Source: Retrieved 26 Jan 2018 from http://www.dailymail.co.uk/news/article-2515929/The-Vegas-Strip-New-cut-steak-discovered-time-10-YEARS.html)

1) Top 20 food trends

- New cuts of meat (e.g. shoulder tender, oyster steak, Vegas Strip Steak, Merlot cut) (See Figure 2-6)

- House-made condiments
- Street food-inspired dishes (e.g. tempura, kabobs, dumplings, pupusas)
- Ethnic-inspired breakfast items (e.g. chorizo scrambled eggs, coconut milk pancakes)
- Sustainable seafood
- Healthful kids' meals
- Vegetable carb substitutes (e.g. cauliflower rice, zucchini spaghetti)
- Uncommon herbs (e.g. chervil, lovage, lemon balm, papalo)
- Authentic ethnic cuisine
- Ethnic spices (e.g. harissa, curry, peri peri, ras el hanout, shichimi)
- Peruvian cuisine
- House-made/artisan pickles
- Heritage-breed meats
- Thai-rolled ice cream
- African flavors
- Ethnic-inspired kids' dishes (e.g. tacos, teriyaki, sushi)
- Donuts with non-traditional filling (e.g. liqueur, Earl Grey cream)
- Gourmet items in kids' meals
- Ethnic condiments (e.g. sriracha, sambal, chimichurri, gochujang, zhug)
- Ancient grains (e.g. kamut, spelt, amaranth, lupin)

2) Top 10 concept trends

- Hyper-local (e.g. restaurant gardens, onsite beer brewing, house-made items)
- Chef-driven fast casual concepts
- Natural ingredients/clean menus
- Food waste reduction

- Veggie-centric/vegetable-forward cuisine (e.g. fresh produce is star of the dish)
- Environmental sustainability
- Locally sourced meat and seafood
- Locally sourced produce
- Simplicity/back to basics
- Farm/estate-branded items

6. Restaurant 2025

"Restaurant 2025" explores artificial intelligence(AI), biometrics/facial recognition/3D imaging, robotics, voice activation, wearable technology, virtual reality, drones, and 3D printing. These new technologies are already changing the way that guests interact with food and beverage operators. The report involves perspectives from more than 250 restaurant operators. The technologies highlighted in "Restaurant 2025" will inevitably redefine the restaurant industry. But whether they yield success depends upon the ability of operators to separate fact from fiction and apply innovations that produce real benefits for consumers and for the business. Here are restaurant operators' top prediction and other top uses (Oracle, 2017). Let's look at it!

■ 60%: Restaurant operators who say restaurant location planning using AI would be mainstream or in mass adoption by 2025.

Operators' other top uses for AI:

- Menu planning based on macro/micro factors
- Waitlist and capacity management

- Dynamic prep time
- Dynamic PAR levels
- Seating planning/forecasting

■ 54%: Restaurant operators who say gathering guest feedback by voice would be mainstream or in mass adoption by 2025.

Operators' other top uses for voice activation/recognition:

- Guest ordering by voice in TSR
- Guest controlling light/ambiance
- Payment by voice
- Guest recognition by voice
- Ordering food at home for delivery by voice

■ 66%: Restaurant operators who say guests paying by wearables would be mainstream or in mass adoption by 2025.

Operators' other top uses for wearable technology:

- Marketing to guests outside the restaurant
- Staff scheduling and training
- Staff check-in to premises and workstations
- Guest recognition
- Staff activity monitoring
- Tailoring menus to guests using their wearables

■ 44%: Restaurant operators who say 3D printing of cutlery/plates would be mainstream or in mass adoption by 2025.

Operators' other top uses for 3D printing:

- 3D printing of furnishings

- Preparing food
- Customizing food

▪ 46%: Restaurant operators who say security by biometrics/facial recognition would be mainstream or in mass adoption by 2025.

Operators' other top uses for Biometrics, Facial Recognition and 3D Imaging:

- Quality control of food
- Food plating/portion control
- Staff scheduling and training
- Guest sentiment measuring
- Staff recognition
- Suggestions to guests based on health/weight
- Guest recognition

▪ 53%: Restaurant operators who say restaurant design/flow optimization via virtual reality would be mainstream or in mass adoption by 2025.

Operators' other top uses for virtual reality:

- Staff training
- Kitchen design
- Guest entertainment
- Enhancing the guest experience

▪ 48%: Restaurant operators who say deliveries to guests' homes by drone would be mainstream or in mass adoption by 2025.

Operators' other top use for drones:

- Deliveries of supplies

Note

- give a peek into : -의 안을 엿보다
- shoulder tender : Shoulder Tender is a relatively unknown cut of Beef. Typically weighing around 8-10 oz (220-280g), this cut is hard to find in the retail market since it is virtually impossible to obtain it as a whole from the carcass.
  Shaped like a pork tenderloin, the Petite Tender Cut is extracted from the Chuck (Shoulder Blade) area of the cow. The cut is also called 'Teres Major', referring to the muscle that it mainly comprises. 'Teres' is a Latin word that means 'rounded', describing the shape of this cut.
  The slices cut off the Shoulder Tender are called 'Medallions' due to their circular appearance.
- oyster steak : 소 엉덩이 뼈 바로 윗 부위 작은 부분
- Vegas Strip Steak : It is hiding in an area of the cow that normally is used for chuck due to its fat, gristle and cartilage.
- merlot cut : 뒷굼치 근육 안쪽 부위
- House-made condiments : 레스토랑에서 직접 만든 양념
- pupusa : A pupusa (Spanish pronunciation: [pu'pusa], from Pipil pupusawa) is a traditional Salvadorean dish of a thick corn tortilla stuffed with a savory filling.
- ethnic-inspired : 에스닉푸드의 영향을 받은
- chorizo : Chorizo is a type of pork sausage.
- Sustainable seafood : Sustainable seafood is seafood that is either caught or farmed in ways that consider the long-term vitality of harvested species and the well-being of the oceans, as well as the livelihoods of fisheries-dependent communities. It was first promoted through the sustainable seafood movement which began in the 1990s. This operation highlights overfishing and environmentally destructive fishing methods. Through a number of initiatives, the movement has increased awareness and raised concerns over the way our seafood is obtained.
- Vegetable carb substitutes : 채소로 탄수화물을 대체하는 것, carb는 carbohydrate(탄수화물)의 약어
- lovage : 러비지는 허브로 분류해야 할지, 향신료로 분류해야 할지, 그도 아니면 채소로 분류해야 할지 난감한 식물이다. 러비지의 향미는 다양한 형태로 수없이 많은 요리

에 쓰인다. 예를 들면 잎은 샐러드에, 씨는 피클에, 줄기는 수프에 넣어 끓인다.

- lemon balm : '멜리사(Melissa)'라고도 불리며 예로부터 밀원 식물로 유명하다. 그리스어로 '밀봉(蜜蜂)'이라는 의미이며, 레몬과 유사한 향이 있다.
- papalo : Papalo is an herbaceous annual plant whose leaves can be used for seasoning food. This plant is known in Mexico as pápaloquelite, commonly accompanying the famous Mexican tacos. Not all Mexicans enjoy its taste, but some find that it improves the flavor of tacos and typical Mexican salsas and soups. In Puebla cuisine, pápalo is used as a condiment on traditional cemita sandwiches, a regional type of Mexican torta.
- harissa : 홍고추로 만든 소스 및 페이스트로 북아프리카 튀니지에서 유래하였다. 아프리카 북서부의 알제리, 모로코, 튀니지, 리비아 일대를 가리키는 마그레브 지역 요리에 많은 영향을 미친 향신료이며, 북아프리카와 중동 요리에 활용된다.
- peri peri : Piri piri is a cultivar of Capsicum chinense, a chili pepper that grows both wild and as a crop. Piri piri sauce를 만드는 주재료로 쓰인다.
- ras el hanout : Ras el hanout or Rass el hanout is a spice mix from North Africa.
- shichimi : Shichi-mi tōgarashi (七味唐辛子, seven-flavor chili pepper), also known as nana-iro tōgarashi (七色唐辛子, seven-color chili pepper) or simply shichimi, is a common Japanese spice mixture containing seven ingredients.
- Heritage breed : Heritage breeds are traditional livestock breeds that were raised by our forefathers. These are the breeds of a bygone era, before industrial agriculture became a mainstream practice. These breeds were carefully selected and bred over time to develop traits that made them well-adapted to the local environment and they thrived under farming practices and cultural conditions that are very different from those found in modern agriculture.
- sriracha : Sriracha is a type of hot sauce or chili sauce made from a paste of chili peppers, distilled vinegar, garlic, sugar, and salt. It is named after the coastal city of Si Racha, in Chonburi Province of eastern Thailand, where it may have been first produced for dishes served at local seafood restaurants.
- sambal : Sambal is a hot sauce or paste typically made from a mixture of a variety of chili peppers with secondary ingredients such as shrimp paste, fish sauce, garlic, ginger, shallot, scallion, palm sugar, lime juice, and rice vinegar or other vinegars. Sambal is an Indonesian loan-word of Javanese origin (sambel). It is native to the cuisines of Indonesia, Malaysia, Sri Lanka, Brunei and Singapore. It has also spread

through overseas Indonesian populations to the Netherlands and Suriname.

- chimichurri : Chimichurri or chimmichurri is an uncooked sauce used for grilled meat; it comes in a green version (chimichurri verde) and a red version (chimichurri rojo) and originates from Argentina and Uruguay. It is made of finely chopped parsley, minced garlic, vegetable oil, oregano, and white vinegar. The dominant flavoring is parsley, garlic, red pepper flakes, and fresh oregano.
- zhug : Zhug, skhug is a Middle Eastern hot sauce originating in Yemeni cuisine. It is very popular in the Arabian Peninsula. Brought to Israel by Yemenite Jews, the condiment is now a staple of Israeli cuisine.
- kamut : 고대 이집트에서 재배되었던 밀의 한 종류. 영양이 풍부하며 씹을수록 고소한 맛이 난다. 셀레늄 등 항산화 성분을 함유하고 있어 미국과 유럽을 중심으로 슈퍼곡물로 주목받고 있다.
- spelt : 스펠트 밀은 57.9%의 탄수화물이 있으며 17%는 단백질, 3%의 지방, 9.2%의 섬유질 등을 함유하고 있다. 글루텐이 많기 때문에 제빵용 가루로도 손색이 없다. 독일에서는 스펠트 밀을 말려서 먹기도 한다.
- amaranth : 남아메리카 안데스산맥의 고산지대에서 약 5,000년 전부터 재배되었던 일년생 비름과 식물로, '신이 내린 곡물'이라고도 불리는 슈퍼푸드 중 하나이다.
- lupin : Eurasian and North African lupins (Lupinus angustifolius) or lupin bean are high in protein, dietary fiber, and antioxidants, very low in starch, and like all legumes, are gluten-free. Lupins can be used to make a variety of foods both sweet and savoury, including everyday meals, traditional fermented foods, baked foods, and sauces.
- Hyper-local : 아주 좁은 범위의 특정 지역에 맞춘 (hyperlocal로도 표기함)
- Chef-driven fast casual concepts : 패스트푸드점에서 셰프가 음식생산에 직접 관여하여 음식의 질을 높인 새로운 서비스 개념
- biometrics : 지문, 홍채, 피부 등 개인의 생체정보를 이용한 인증 방식
- voice activation : (IT) <위성통신>음성 구동(音聲驅動)
- top prediction : 최상의 예측
- top uses : 최상의 활용도
- PAR levels : Par levels are the ideal amount of inventory you want in stock after you place an order. Setting up par levels is a great way to improve your ordering efficiency and effectiveness.
- TSR : Table Service Restaurant, cf) QSR: Quick Service Restaurant

References

Butler, Richard V. and Mary E. Stefl, 2008, "The ECONOMIC IMPACT of San Antonio's HOSPITALITY INDUSTRY," San Antonio Area Tourism Council, Retrieved Jan. 16, 2010 from http://www.sariverfoundation.org/downloads/visitor_study.pdf/benchmark/2009/html/naicsdef.html

Colorado Restaurant Association, "Hospitality News," Feb 2017, Retrieved Jan. 5, 2018 from http://www.coloradorestaurant.com/admin/includes/js/kcfinder/upload/file/CRA-February 2017Newsletter.pdf

Ctculinary, "Fast Track to Culinary Career Success," Retrieved Jan. 14, 2010 from http://www.ctculinary.com/careerpaths/index.htm

Dailymail, "New cut of steak discovered for the first time in 10 YEARS: Meat expert unveils the 'Vegas Strip' cut from obscure area of shoulder," 2018, Retrieved Jan. 5, 2018 from http://www.dailymail.co.uk/news/article-2515929/The-Vegas-Strip-New-cut-steak-discovered-time-10-YEARS.html

Jamrisko, Michelle, "Americans' Spending on Dining Out Just Overtook Grocery Sales for the First Time Ever," Retrieved Jan. 5, 2018 from https://www.bloomberg.com/news/articles/2015-04-14/americans-spending-out-just-overtook-grocery-sales-for-the-first-time-ever

Livecareer, 2009, "Careers in the Culinary Industry Draw Spotlight," Sep. 11, Retrieved Jan. 14, 2010 from http://www.livecareer.com/news/Travel-Entertainment-Culinary/Careers-in-the-Culinary-Industry-Draw-Spotlight_$$01002.aspx,

NRA, "2017 Restaurant Industry POCKET FACEBOOK," Retrieved Jan. 2, 2018 from https://www.restaurant.org/Downloads/PDFs/News-Research/Pocket_Factbook_FEB_2017-FINAL.pdf

NRA, "Restaurant Industry 2017 and Beyond," May 20, 2017, Retrieved Jan. 2, 2018 from https://www.restaurant.org/Downloads/PDFs/Events-Groups/Fast-Casual-Show-State-of-Industry-Presentation-Ma.pdf

NRA, "What's Hot for Menu Trends in 2018," December 8, 2017, Retrieved Jan. 2,2018 from https://www.preparedfoods.com/articles/120702-whats-hot-for-menu-trends-in-2018

Oracle, "Restaurant 2025," 2017, Retrieved Jan. 2, 2018 from https://www.oracle.com/web folder/s/delivery_production/docs/FY16h1/doc36 /Restaurant-2025-Oracle-Hospitality.pdf

QSR magazine as of August 20, 2015, accessed on August 31, 2015; Franchise Helpaccessed on September 1, 2015; Nerac accessed on September 1, 2015; PR Newswire as of August 10, 2015, accessed on August 31, 2015, Ibid., KPMG, "An appetite for change," Retrieved Jan. 5, 2018 from https://assets.kpmg.com /content/dam/kpmg/pdf/2016/07/An-Appetite-For-Change.pdf

Sealover, Ed, "7 chefs make $7.4 million economic impact in booming Denver restaurant industry," Oct 10, 2015, Retrieved Jan. 5, 2018 from https://www.bizjournals.om/denver /cnews/2015/10/09/7-chefs-make-7-4-million-economic-impact-in.html

Tellefsen, Robyn, "A Sampling of the Culinary Industry," Retrieved Jan. 14, 2010 from http://www.degrees-in-culinary.com/article/a-sampling-of-the-culinary-industry/890/

Retrieved Jan. 3, 2018 from https://www.bls.gov/ooh/food-preparation-and-serving/chefs-and-head-cooks.htm

Retrieved Jan. 3, 2018 from https://www.bls.gov/oes/current/oes351011.htm

Retrieved Jan. 3, 2018 from https://www1.salary.com/Executive-Chef-Salary.html

Retrieved Jan. 3, 2018 from https://www.workbc.ca/careers/6321#bc-labour-market-outlook

Retrieved Jan. 3, 2018 from https://www.bizjournals.com/denver/news/2015/10/09/7-chefs-make -7-4-million-economic-impact-in.html

Retrieved Jan. 3, 2018 from http://www.sariverfoundation.org/downloads/visitor_study.pdf

Retrieved Jan. 14, 2018 from https://livestockconservancy.org/index.php/heritage

Retrieved Jan. 14, 2018 from http://nosetotailapp.com/meat-cuts/beef/shoulder-tender

Retrieved Jan. 13, 2018 from http://encarta.msn.com/encnet/features/dictionary/

Retrieved Jan. 14, 2018 from http://education.yahoo.com/,

Retrieved Jan. 14, 2018 from http://www.merriam-webster.com/,

Chapter 03

Career Guide

Description : MCGUIRE AIR FORCE BASE, N.J. - Staff Sgt. Kevin Casciano, a chef with the 305th Services Squadron, and Emeril Lagasse discuss meals ready to eat during the Sept. 25 taping of the celebrity chef's Thanksgiving special here. The show is scheduled to air Nov. 16. Check local listings for times.

(Source : Retrieved 26 Jan 2018 from http://www.af.mil/News/Article-Display/Article/138454/emeril-salutes-troops-at-mcguire/)

"If an architect makes a mistake, he grows ivy to cover it. If a doctor makes a mistake, he covers it with soil. If a cook makes a mistake, he covers it with some sauce and says it is a new recipe."

- Paul Bocuse (11 February 1926 – 20 January 2018), a French chef

1. Why Study Culinary Arts?

It is not often that one can take something he or she loves and build it into a career. However, that is the case with culinary arts. Those who love to cook can take this avocation and build it into a vocation, provided they have the stamina to keep up with the rigorous pace of this occupation.

Are you passionate about food and the culinary industry? Have you thought that you can turn this into a successful career? The food service industry is growing rapidly, and culinary professionals are in great demand. Studying culinary arts is important since students acquire the necessary skills to start working in this challenging field. Below you can see more reasons why a career in culinary arts is a good choice for the future (B.H.M.S., n.d.).

1) Learn how to cook and make the dishes attractive

You can develop skills in food preparation and presentation. During the course, you join classes in which you learn the principles of food pairing (which ingredients match) and the art of food plating (presentation techniques).

2) Entrepreneurship

A degree in culinary arts provides the knowledge of restaurant management and business basics, especially useful for those who want to run their own culinary or catering business. You can also use your knowledge to other professions related to food, such as food stylist.

3) Work in the world's finest dining establishments

If you want to become a chef, attending a culinary school is the beginning of your career. Education combined with experience is the best formula to acquire success! You can boost your career as soon as you have developed your skills better, and you can have the opportunity to work in many top-level restaurants.

4) Try new flavors

Explore regional and international cuisines and prepare a range of international popular dishes.

5) Travel the world

This career can lead you in working abroad. With your knowledge, you can be specialized to work in establishments around the world.

6) Learn new languages and cultures

Studying culinary arts abroad will expose you to new languages and cultures. Food is one of the ways we experience and understand other cultures. You will also be able to express yourself differently in the kitchen, and it may inspire your creative side.

2. Culinary Training and Education

1) Formal Training and Education

To succeed as a culinary professional, he or she should obtain formal training and education through an accredited culinary school. When it comes to working in the top tier of the culinary industry, a person will benefit the most from earning a bachelor's degree or higher. Such degree programs tend to center on a wide range of culinary-related topics as well as the following: food service entrepreneurship, restaurant management, food service management, and hospitality.

If you want to earn a formal education, you should spend a lot of time taking part in hands-on training. Some culinary programs will mandate that a student complete an apprenticeship or internship under a trained culinary professional before graduation. The hands-on training portion of a culinary program can usually be completed through a wide range of outlets, including hotels, spas, casinos, country clubs, restaurants and more.

2) Certification

It can be very advantageous to earn a culinary diploma or degree, and earning a certificate is very advantageous as well. This type of credential is required by some dining establishments. When it comes to certifications, ACF(American Culinary Federation) offers the following: (CEC) Certified Executive Chef, (PPC) Personal Certified Chef, (CC) Certified Culinarian, (CMC) Certified Master Chef, (CSC) Certified Sous Chef, (PCEC) Personal Certified Executive Chef, and (CCC) Certified Chef de Cuisine (Zacparker, 2013).

3. Job Prospects

Before getting into the world of culinary industry, three aspects must be considered. Those aspects are opportunities, weaknesses, and traits/talents. The first 2 aspects are inevitable characteristics that culinary industry has, and the other aspect is one that young students must develop and have while in a college or an university.

1) Opportunities

Coming straight out of cooking school, most starting chefs are able easily to find work in the culinary field, allowing them to hone their skills as they continue to build fine careers in the culinary industry. People will always need food for theirsurvival, and as long as there are appetites, people will seek better and more interesting foods to appease their palate. You can be the chef that fulfills those needs (Culinaryed, n.d.).

A restaurant, however, is by no means the only option for a work environment. There are plentiful opportunities for chefs outside of the restaurant setting. You could work in hospitality, on a cruise or at a resort; as an industry chef in the kitchens of schools, businesses, hospitals, cafeterias, and other institutions; as a personal chef in someone's home; you could specialize as a pastry chef or baker; the possibilities are endless. For these reasons it is difficult to pin down the general job description of someone working in the culinary field. However, that can be good news because it means that unique opportunities abound (Careereducationadvisor, n.d.).

Most people eat three times a day, and when they are not actively eating, they are considering what and where their next meal will be. Most industries do not experience this sort of stability when it comes to the demand for their products. The culinary industry is one of the fastest growing industries in the world. The culinary industry itself can be just as diverse as the professionals it's comprised of. The culinary industry is unique because, as long as you create a dish that appeals to at least a small segment of the population, you are bound to be successful. In fact, the culinary industry can be the excellent place to start and make your living (Careereducationadvisor, n.d.; Smith, 2009).

While television shows and magazines have helped popularize this field in recent years, many of these would-be chefs come into the business as a second career. People who have a passion for food and cooking are good candidates for working in the culinary industry. If you are one of those who love spending time in preparing different foods or like to work with people in food decoration then making a career in the culinary industry can surely be the most appropriate decision (Smith, 2009, Articlesbase, 2009). From positions in restaurants, resorts, spas and cruise lines to careers in nutrition, food product development or as a celebrity chef—opportunities in the expansive culinary industry are limited only by your imagination (Jwu, 2008).

2) Weaknesses

Many restaurant and institutional kitchens have modern equipment, convenient work areas, and air conditioning, but kitchens in older and smaller eating places are often not as well designed. Kitchen staffs invariably work in small quarters against hot stoves and ovens. They are under constant pressure to prepare meals quickly, while ensuring quality is maintained and safety and sanitation guidelines are observed (Newfuturesdc, 2009).

The culinary industry does not adhere to a 9 to 5 schedule, five days a week. Work hours in the culinary industry may include early mornings, late evenings, holidays, and weekends. In particular the weekend evening hours are the boom time in the culinary industry. In order to become a successful master chef, you must be available and at your best during the culinary industry's peak hours. Serving a fine meal for dinner is one of the main goals, and this often makes life difficult for those with families or loved ones. Many executive chefs regularly work 12-hour days because they oversee the delivery of foodstuffs early in the day, plan the menu, and prepare those menu items that take the most skill (Newfuturesdc, 2009). In order to become a successful chef, you must be able to work around such obstacles and resign yourself to living outside of the weekend (Culinaryed, n.d.).

3) Traits/Talents

You must be highly organized in order to schedule food preparation, coordinate the work of the kitchen staff, and ensure that quality food supplies are available in the right quantities. In addition, you should be people-oriented and a team player, as you will be working closely with kitchen and service staff. Chefs are often caught in stressful situations, but you must remain courteous, tactful, patient and calm.

As the presentation of a meal is almost as important as the preparation of its ingredients, you should have a creative and artistic flair. A keen sense of taste and smell are also necessary, as is good hand-eye coordination. Since you will be handling food for a large portion of the day, you need to exhibit high standards of personal hygiene and cleanliness (Skillsalberta, 2009).

Note

- avocation : a hobby or minor occupation
- entrepreneurship : the state of being an entrepreneur, or the activities associated with being an entrepreneur
- accredited : certified or guaranteed as meeting required standards
- hands-on : involving practical experience of equipment, etc
- aspect : one part of a situation, problem, subject, etc
- trait : a particular characteristic that can produce a particular type of behaviour
- appease : to satisfy or relieve
- palate : a person's ability to taste and judge good food and wine
- pin sth down : to discover exact details about something
- abound : to exist in large numbers
- bound : (after verb) certain or extremely likely to happen
- would-be : wanting or trying to be
- celebrity : someone who is famous, especially in the entertainment business
- quarter : an area of a town where a particular group of people live or work or where a particular activity happens
- adhere to sth : to continue to obey a rule or have a belief
- obstacle : something that blocks you so that movement, going forward or action are prevented or made more difficult
- resign yourself to sth : to make yourself accept something that you do not like because you cannot change it
- courteous : polite and respectful; well-mannered
- tactful : careful not to say or do anything that could upset someone
- flair : natural ability to do something well
- hand-eye coordination : the ability to do things that involve your hands and eyes working together, for example catching a ball, passing something through a needle, or drawing pictures
- coordination : the act of making all the people involved in a plan or activity work together in an organized way
- hygiene : the degree to which people keep themselves or their environment clean, especially to prevent disease

4. Building a Career in the Culinary Industry

The culinary industry has and will continue to have excellent job opportunities. Millions of meals are prepared daily in restaurants, hotels, schools, and health care facilities. Upon graduation from professional culinary programs at a culinary College or University, you will be able to pursue a number of rewarding careers. The possibilities are endless. Many of the following career opportunities are available for students completing an associate degree in culinary arts. Just think what you could do with an associate's degree or a bachelor's degree! Let's start a new career in the culinary industry.

1) Career opportunities involving cooking

① Chef Owners (Chef patron) : Some chefs open their own restaurants or other types of food service establishments. However running a successful business requires another set of skills such as leadership skills, strategic business planning skills, marketing skills, customer skills(sales, service and customer relationship management), communication skills, people management skills, and finance and accounting skills (Smallbusinesspro, 2018). Chefs who want to open their own restaurants should cultivate knowledge in management, marketing, and accounting (Howtobecome, 2018).

Perhaps some day young students, who are experienced, highly motivated persons and learn knowledge about costs, marketing, and the more which are requisite for a restaurant's success, will have its own Michelin-starred chef-owned restaurant.

② Executive Chefs : They are in charge of all kitchen staff and the meals that are prepared. They oversee all kitchen operations and handle duties such as ordering supplies, keeping accounts, and planning menus. They are also responsible for food preparation and styling, recipe development, and meal creation. Executive chefs ensure appealing presentation as well as good taste. In large restaurants with numerous staff, executive chefs may do little of the actual cooking. But they work long hours nevertheless (Cookingschools, n.d.).

③ Baking & Pastry Chefs (Dessert Specialist, Bread and Pastry Baker, Pastry Chef or Patissier) : The pastry chef prepares pastries and desserts, as well as bread and other baked goods. In larger restaurants, pastry chefs may supervise a pastry team in a separate kitchen. Pastry chefs are often in charge of the dessert menu, and will research, create, and test new recipes. They may also oversee other dessert-related items, such as dessert wines, dessert beverages, and gourmet cheese platters (Edu.chefsblade, n.d.).

④ Food Preparation and Serving Supervisors : They oversee the kitchen and non-kitchen staff in a restaurant or food service facility. They may also oversee food preparation workers in fast food, cafeteria, or casual dining restaurants, where the menu is fairly standard from day to day, or in more formal restaurants, where a chef provides specific guidelines and exacting standards on how to prepare each item (Careers.collegetoolkit, n.d.).

⑤ Institutional Chefs : Institutional chefs work in the kitchens of schools, industrial cafeterias, hospitals, and other institutions. For each meal, they prepare a small selection of entrees, vegetables, and desserts, but in large quantities (edonline, n.d.)

⑥ Personal Chefs (Private Household Cooks, Private Chefs, Freelance Chefs) :

A personal chef is someone who is a trained cook, who prepares at-home meals for their clients for a fee. Personal chefs are usually employed by one family or one household; they will customize a meal plan according to the client's dietary needs and preferences, shop for the items, prepare the meal, and also clean up the kitchen after they're done. This saves their clients the time and effort needed to cook their own food, which can be very valuable to people that are extremely busy (sokanu.com, n.d.).

⑦ Catering Chefs (Caterers and Event Planners, Catering Specialists) : Some caterers own their own businesses, while others have managerial positions in hotel and resort catering operations. They provide services, food and beverages for various types of social functions. They design the perfect menus for a function or event, such as a wedding, company party, conference, intimate dinner or other type of social gatherings. Some caterers specialize in a specific type of food, while others specialize in foods for a specific type of event. Many catering chefs cross over the entire spectrum of styles in an effort to work in a variety of situations. They need to be able to produce large amounts of scrumptious food. They should also have good communication skills to collaborate on menus with their clients. Many catering chefs obtain certification through a culinary institute or technical school (Degreedirectory, n.d.; Baker, n.d.).

⑧ Food Stylists : A food stylist is someone who showcases food for photography, video, or film. Making food photogenic is not as easy as one may think, and the best food stylists come to the job armed with a variety of tools and techniques to make food look both beautiful and appetizing (sokanu, n.d.)

2) Career opportunities not involving cooking

Not all positions of employment for culinary arts professionals involve cooking. Here are some examples.

① Restaurateurs (Restaurant Owners) : They own and manage a restaurant (dictionary.cambridge, n.d.). The Cornell University School of Hotel Administration confirms that the most successful restaurateurs have a clear concept and the ability to implement it consistently, as well as the determination to succeed and the flexibility to adapt to changing market conditions (including economic downturns) (Sandlin, 2007).

② Food Writers (Cookbook Authors, Food Critics, Blogger) : They establish a public contact with the public on food trends, chefs and restaurants. Many write for newspapers, magazines and some publish books. Notables in this field include Julia Child, Craig Claiborne and James Beard (Directoryofschools, n.d.).

③ Entrepreneurs : They are self-motivated persons who run a business (Patel, 2016). They develop their own business with examples including restaurants, bakeries, specialty food manufacture (chocolates, cheese etc) (Directoryofschools, n.d.).

④ Media Personalities (TV personality, Television personality) : They deliver all the information and entertainment services based on culinary activities to the home.

⑤ Food Service Managers (Restaurant Managers) : They are responsible for the daily operations of restaurants and other establishments that prepare and serve meals and beverages to customers. Besides coordinating activities among various departments, such as kitchen, dining room, and banquet operations, food service managers ensure that customers are satisfied with their dining experience. In addition, they oversee the inventory and ordering of food, equipment, and supplies and arrange for the routine maintenance and upkeep of the restaurant's equipment and facilities. Managers are generally responsible for all administrative and human-resource functions of the business, including recruiting new employees and monitoring employee performance and training (Bis, 2009),

⑥ Food and Beverage Managers (Food and Beverage Supervisors, Wines & Spirits Specialists) : They manage all food and beverage outlets in hotels and other large establishments (Directoryofschools, n.d.).

⑦ Food and Beverage Controllers (Purchasing Agents) : They purchase and source ingredients in large hotels as well as manage the stores and stock control (Directoryofschools, n.d.).

⑧ Consultants (Food Consultants, Design specialists, Restaurant Designers, Kitchen Designers) : They works with restaurant owners in development of menus, layout and design of dining room and establishing kitchen protocols (Directoryofschools, n.d.).

⑨ Salespeople (Sales Representatives) : They introduce chefs and business owners to new products and are able to demonstrate the proper use at equipment. They may sell any range at products needed in the industry from various food products to equipment (Directoryofschools, n.d.).

⑩ Educators (Instructors) : Chef instructors train aspiring chefs in high school vocational programs, vocational schools, and colleges. They give lectures and demonstrations, assign homework, and guide skill labs. Chef instructors need to develop lesson plans, interact and/or collaborate with fellow teachers, assess students' skills through exams and demonstrations of abilities, meet with and advise individual students, and stay informed about the latest trends in the field (Study.com, n.d.).

⑪ Research & Development Directors (Research and Development Chefs, Menu Development Chefs, Recipe/Food Tester) : They develop new products for commercial manufacturers, manage test kitchens for publications or kitchens for restaurant chains or grocery chains (Directoryofschools, n.d.).

⑫ Culinologists : Culinology® is the blending of the culinary arts and the science of food. Originally, the word was designed to be a combination of two words: "culinary" and "technology". Culinologists work in diverse aspects of food—from experimental chefs and menu planners to food manufacturing to fine dining. The word is protected by the professional association, the Research Chefs Association, which owns the registered trademark (Wikipedia, 2017).

Note

- requisite : an important necessary thing
- acclaim : public approval and praise
- entail : to make something necessary, or to involve something
- oversee : to watch or organize a job or an activity to make certain that it is being done correctly
- platter : a large plate used for serving food or a meal with one type of food served on a large plate
- function : an official ceremony or a formal social event, such as a party or a special meal, at which a lot of people are usually present
- intimate : having, or being likely to cause, a very close friendship or personal or sexual relationship
- gathering : a party or a meeting when many people come together as a group
- scrumptious : tasting extremely pleasant; delicious
- collaborate : to work with someone else for a special purpose
- upkeep : the cost or process of keeping something, such as a building, in good condition
- administrative : relating to the arrangements and work which is needed to control the operation of a plan or organization
- recruit : to persuade someone to work for a company or become a new member of an organization, especially the army
- monitor : to watch and check a situation carefully for a period of time in order to discover something about it
- outlet : shop that is one of many owned by a particular company and that sells the goods which the company has produced
- source : to get something from a particular place
- protocol : the rules of correct or appropriate behavior of a group, organization, or profession

References

Bis, 2009, "Food Service Managers Occupational Outlook Handbook," 2010-11 Edition, December 17, Retrieved Jan. 14, 2010 from http://www.bls.gov/oco/ocos024.htm

Business Skills to Run Your Own Business, Retrieved Jan. 4, 2018 from http://www.smallbusinesspro.co.uk/start-business/business-skills.html

Careereducationadvisor, "Profile: Culinary Industry," Retrieved Jan. 14, 2010 from http://www.careereducationadvisor.com/Profile-Culinary-Industry.htm

Careers.collegetoolkit, "Chefs and Head Cooks," Retrieved Jan. 14, 2010 from http://careers.collegetoolkit.com/careers/chefs_and_head_cooks/tasks/35-1011.00.aspx

Cookingschools, "Executive Chef," Retrieved Jan. 14, 2010 from http://www.cookingschools.com/cooking-culinary-careers/executive-chef.html

Culinaryed, "Becoming a Skilled Chef." Retrieved Jan. 9, 2010 from http://www.culinaryed.com/

Degreedirectory, "Catering Chef: Become a Catering Chef in 5 Steps," Retrieved Jan. 14, 2010 from http://degreedirectory.org/articles/Catering_Chef_Become_a_Catering_Chef_in_5_Steps.html

Directoryofschools, "Campus Programs," Retrieved Jan. 14, 2010 from http://www.directoryofschools.com/LEcole-Culinaire/Culinary-Arts.htm

Edonline, "Chefs, Cooks, and Other Kitchen Workers," Retrieved Jan. 4, 2018 from http://www.edonline.com/collegecompass/oohb0177.htm

Edu.chefsblade, "Cooking Career Specialties," Retrieved Jan. 14, 2010 from http://edu.chefsblade.com/v/main/articles/2331-cooking-career-specialties_cs

How to Become a Chef, Retrieved Jan. 4, 2018 from https://www.howtobecome.com/how-to-become-a-chef

Jwu, 2008, "College Of Culinary Arts," Retrieved Dec. 27, 2009 from http://www.jwu.edu/college.aspx?id=30742

Newfuturesdc, 2009, 2009-2010 Career Guide; Promising Careers that Don't Require Four

Years of College, New Futures, Retrieved Feb. 5, 2010 from http://www.newfuturesdc.org/wp-content/uploads/2009/11/Career-Guide.pdf

Patel, Neil, "The 7 Secrets Self-Motivated Entrepreneurs Know," Retrieved Jan. 5, 2018 from https://www.entrepreneur.com/article/251591

Sandlin, Eileen Figure, "The Ingredients of Restaurant Success," March 1, 2007, Retrieved Jan. 8, 2018 from https://www.entrepreneur.com/article/174770

Skillsalberta, 2009, "34 CULINARY ARTS," Retrieved Jan. 9, 2010 from http://www.skillsalberta.com/pdf/promomaterial/SchoolTours2.pdf

Smith, Anne Kates, 2009, "Seasoned to Taste: Culinary Industry Opportunities Comein Many Flavors," Jul. 26, Retrieved Jan. 14, 2010 from http://educo.uber.matchbin.net/printer_friendly/3035068

Smsu, "Culinology," 2010, Jan. 10, Retrieved Jan. 14, 2010 from http://www.smsu.edu/Academics/Programs/Culinology/Index.cfm?Id=795&output=pdf

Sokanu, "What does a Personal Chef do?," Retrieved Jan. 4, 2018 from https://www.sokanu.com/careers/personal-chef/

Study.com, "How to Become a Chef Instructor: Education and Career Roadmap,"Retrieved Jan. 4, 2019 from https://study.com/articles/How_to_Become_a_Chef_Instructor_Education_and_Career_Roadmap.html

Zacparker, "The Secret Guide to Culinary Career," Jul 1, 2013, Retrieved Jan. 7,2018 from https://cheftalk.com/ams/the-secret-guide-to-culinary-career.27998/

Retrieved Jan. 3, 2018 from https://en.oxforddictionaries.com/definition/us/avocation

Retrieved Jan. 3, 2018 from http://encarta.msn.com/

Retrieved Jan. 3, 2018 from http://www.merriam-webster.com/dictionary/

Retrieved Jan. 7, 2018 from https://dictionary.cambridge.org/

Retrieved Jan. 7, 2018 from https://en.wikipedia.org/wiki/Culinology

Retrieved Jan. 7, 2018 from https://www.sokanu.com/careers/food-stylist/

Retrieved Jan. 7, 2018 from https://study.com/articles/How_to_Become_a_Chef_Instructor_Education_and_Career_Roadmap.html

Chapter 04

Positive Attitude toward the Culinary Industry

Description : Staff Sgt. Ma Antonette Cabantog prepares hors d'oeuvre during a dinner engagement hosted by the Chairman of the Joint Chief of Staff Martin Dempsey.
(Source : Retrieved 26 Jan 2018 from http://airman.dodlive.mil/2017/01/23/recipe-for-success/)

"Some people like to paint pictures, or do gardening, or build a boat in the basement. Other people get a tremendous pleasure out of the kitchen, because cooking is just as creative and imaginative an activity as drawing, or wood carving, or music."

- Julia Child (August 15, 1912 – August 13, 2004), an American chef, author and television personality

1. I am A Chef!

When the author was preparing materials for editing "Guide to the Culinary Industry," this poem was found at www.globalchefs.com in Jan. 10, 2004 and downloaded from the website, but now its domain has expired. Jema Emawrote this poem whose title is "I am a chef." As you can see from the content, It is a poem about having a career.

I am a chef; every day I waked up tired.
I am a chef; every day my feet are sore.
I am a chef; every day I ride the bus with workers who will finish at five.
I am a chef; and today I will skip my break.
I am a chef; every day sweat stings my eyes.
I am a chef; every day I deal with bullshit.
I am a chef; every day I fight waiters.
I am a chef; I have scares to prove it.
I am a chef; every day I peel, chop, and slice.
I am a chef; every day I learn, teach, and create.
I am a chef; every day I reach a natural high.
I am a chef, and at the end of every day—I am proud of what I do.

2. Culinary Laboratory Uniform and Code of Conduct Policy

This is part of culinary laboratory uniform and code of conduct policy used in a college in the United States. It is a typical example of uniform and personal hygiene code and lab requirements. You must follow these code and requirements just after this course. Let's explore it (Algonquin College, 2016).

Description : Chef's preparing a seafood paella in Playa del Carmen, Mexico
(Source: Retrieved 26 Jan 2018 from https://commons.wikimedia.org/wiki/File:Chefs.jpg)

1) Uniforms

All students must be properly dressed in a chef's uniform for the lab classes. Students are required to wear college approved uniform items. Full uniform will include chef check pants, chef jacket, neck tic, apron, side towels, hat, name tag and shoes. Students should enter and leave the lab class in uniform. Uniforms must be complete, clean, stain-free, and wrinkle-free prior to every class.

All chef's coats are to be buttoned to the top button and sleeves worn down. Changing in the kitchen or hall way is not permitted. Professional appearance must be maintained throughout the campus at all times while in uniform. Complete uniforms are required for the first day of a food lab class. If a T-shirt is worn under your chef jacket it should be plain white with no logos. Chef pants must be hemmed.

2) Personal Hygiene

Students are required to practice and demonstrate a strict level of personal hygiene in the laboratory classes. Use of strong fragrances are prohibited. Use of deodorant is required. Fingernails must be kept short, clean and free of any type of nail covering, such as: nail polish, artificial nails, etc.

All hair, short or long, must remain neatly cut and restrained at all times. All long hair (hair touching the collar of the chef's jacket) must be pulled up and restrained by the chef's hat. In some cases hair nets may be required. Hair past the collar of your jacket must be restrained. Students should be clean-shaven. If facial hair is present it must be trimmed and kept at a short acceptable length.

3) Shoes

Students are required to wear college approved footwear. Black Socks must be worn with shoes. Stockings are not acceptable or safe in the kitchen.

4) Jewellery

No jewellery except the following may by worn in labs: wedding and engagement rings. wrist watch. one set of post earrings in the ears that are not large or dangling.

5) Kitchen Tool Requirements

All students must have full tool kits before commencement of culinary labs. Attendance to all classes is mandatory. Culinary Labs are presented in sequence. Each lab consists of a set of skills that are necessary for successfully completing the course. If a student does not meet the attendance requirement for that class, the student will not successfully complete the course. The student will be allowed to continue to attend class however; the grading of the student will stop by the instructor. It is required for you to arrive to the labs at least 10 minutes prior to the beginning of the class.

The instructor has a right to ask the student to wait outside if the student's lateness will cause disruption to the demonstration or the lecture. It is the responsibility of the student to acquire the information that was missed during their absence. If an absence or lateness is foreseeable it is the responsibility of the student to communicate to the chef instructor via email or phone call, before the beginning of class.

6) Lab Clean Up and Set Up

All students should work in a professional, clean and organized manner at all times.No student shall leave the class before clean-up of the labs are complete.

Anyone who leaves will be subjected to academic penalty. It is the responsibility of the students to keep the dishwashing area clean and organized at all times. Students should follow "clean as you go" procedure. Each student is responsible for cleaning and washing their own dishes and sanitizing. All dishes must still be rinsed and sanitized in the designated dishwashing area.

Students are required to wash and sanitize their respective work areas and cutting boards in the beginning and at the end of each lab. Sanitizer should also be used as needed during the lab and should be located in each working area.

All stations will be set up according to chef's instruction. The storage shelves must be clean and organized after every lab. All the dishes and small ware will be washed and dried before being placed on the shelf. The compost is required to be changed as needed during the class. It is the responsibility of the group to change the garbage who is assigned the garbage duty as per cleaning schedule. Recycling must be sorted by each student and put into their respective bins.

Note

- laboratory : (informal lab) a room or place with appropriate equipment for teaching science or doing scientific work
- code : a set of principles that are accepted and used by society or a particular group of people
- hygiene : the degree to which people keep themselves or their environment clean, especially to prevent disease
- checkered : patterned with alternating squares of color
- staine : a mark left accidentally on clothes or surfaces
- hem : to fold the edge of a piece of cloth and sew it in place

- fragrance : a perfume (=a liquid with a pleasant smell that people put on their skin).
- deodorant : a substance that you put on your skin to prevent your body from having an unpleasant smell
- polish : a substance used to make something smooth or shiny
- foreseeable : able to be foreseen or predicted

3. Professionalism

No matter what your co-worker's attitudes, your professionalism demonstrates to others a level of commitment and a personal focus on excellence. What does it mean to be a professional? Consider the following list (Larousse, 1996).

Elements of Professionalism

① Focus on the job at hand, and perform all tasks and responsibilities to the best of your ability.

② Wear clean and well-pressed proper attire, and maintain good personal hygiene.

③ Practice being a good listener. (This promotes teamwork, esprit de corps, and camaraderie.)

④ Avoid profanity, crude jokes, and gossip. No matter how tough things are, make an effort to accentuate the positive.

⑤ Remember, the culinary industry is a service industry. Customer-oriented service is the best advertising for any service business.

⑥ Learn to wind down after each work day by cultivating conversation with friends and co-workers, reading, and other constructive activities.

⑦ Establish a steadfast rule: Never consume alcohol during a work shift.

⑧ Physically demanding work does not take the place of healthful exercise. Set aside time weekly to maintain good physical fitness.

⑨ Do all things in moderation. (It takes 21 consecutive days to develop a new habit.)

⑩ Arrive at work punctually and stay until the last customer is served.

Note

- Professionalism : the high standard that you expect from a person who is well trained in a particular job
- attire : clothes
- maintain : to make sth continue at the same level, standard, etc.
- hygiene : the practice of keeping yourself and your living and working areas clean in order to prevent illness and disease
- esprit de corps : (from French) feelings of pride, care and support for each other, etc. that are shared by the members of a group
- camaraderie : a feeling of friendship and trust among people who work or spend a lot of time together
- profanity : swear words, or religious words used in a way that shows a lack of respect for God or holy things
- accentuate : to emphasize sth or make it more noticeable
- positive : a good or useful quality or aspect
- wind down : to rest or relax after a period of activity or excitement
- steadfast : not changing in your attitudes or aims

- set aside : to save or keep money or time for a particular purpose in moderation
- adhere to : to behave according to a particular law, rule, set of instructions, etc.; to follow a particular set of beliefs or a fixed way of doing sth
- profession : a type of job that needs special training or skill, especially one that needs a high level of education
- enlightenment : knowledge about and understanding of sth; the process of understanding sth or making sb understand it
- get in the way of : to prevent sb from doing sth; to prevent sth from happening
- communal : shared by, or for the use of, a number of people, especially people who live together

4. Standards of Professionalism

The emphasis of a food service education is on learning a set of skills. But in many ways, attitudes are more important than skills because a good attitude will help you not only learn skills but also persevere and overcome the many difficulties you will face in your career. The successful food service worker follows an unwritten code of behavior and set of attitudes we call professionalism. Let's look at some of the qualities that a professional must have (Larousse, 1996).

① Positive attitude toward the job

In order to be a good professional cook, you have to like cooking and want to do it well. Being serious about your work doesn't mean you can't enjoy it. But the enjoyment comes from the satisfaction of doing your job well and making everything run smoothly.

Every experienced chef knows the stimulation of the rush. When it's the busiest time of the evening, the orders are coming in so fast you can hardly keep track of them, and every split second counts—then, when everyone digs in and works together and everything clicks, there's real excitement in the air. But this excitement comes only when you work for it.

A cook with a positive attitude works quickly, efficiently, neatly, and safely. Professionals have pride in their work and want to make sure that the work is something to be proud of.

② Staying power

Food service requires physical and mental stamina, good health, and a willingness to work hard. It is hard work. The pressures can be intense and the hours long and grueling. You may be working evenings and weekends when everyone else is playing. And the work can be monotonous. You might think it's drudgery to hand-shape two or three dozen dinner rolls for your baking class, but wait until you get that job in the big hotel and are told to make 3000 canapés for a party.

③ Ability to work with people

Few of you will work in an establishment so small that you are the only person on the staff. Food service work is teamwork, and it's essential to be able to work well on a team and to cooperate with your fellow workers. You can't afford to let ego problems, petty jealousy, departmental rivalries, or feelings about other people get in the way of doing the job well. In the old days, many chefs were famous for their temper tantrums. Fortunately, self-control is more valued today.

④ Eagerness to learn

There is more to learn about cooking than you will learn in a lifetime. But isn't it great to try? The greatest chefs in the world are the first to admit that they have more to learn, and they keep working, experimenting, and studying. The food service industry is changing so rapidly that it is vital to be open to new ideas. No matter how good your techniques are, you might learn an even better way.

⑤ A full range of skills

Most people who become professional cooks do so because they like to cook. This is an important motivation, but it is also important to develop and maintain other skills that are necessary for the profession. To be successful, a cook must understand and manage food cost and other financial matters, manage and maintain proper inventories, deal with purveyors, and understand personnel management.

⑥ Experience

One of the most respected chefs has said, "You don't really know how to cook a dish until you have done it a thousand times." There is no substitute for years of experience. Studying cooking principles in books and in schools can get your career off to a running start. You may learn more about basic cooking theories from your chef instructors than you could in several years of working your way up from washing vegetables. But if you want to become an accomplished cook, you need practice, practice, and more practice. A diploma will not make you a chef.

⑦ Dedication to quality

Many people think that only a special category of food can be called gourmet food. It's hard to say exactly what that is. Apparently, the only thing so-called gourmet foods have in common is high price.

The only distinction worth making is between well-prepared food and poorly prepared food. There is good roast duckling à l'orange and there is bad roast duckling à l'orange. There are good hamburgers and French fries, and there are bad hamburgers and French fries.

Whether you work in a fancy French restaurant, a fast-food restaurant, a college cafeteria, or a catering house, you can do your job well, or not. The choice is yours.

High quality doesn't necessarily mean high price. It costs no more to cook green beans properly than to overcook them. But in order to produce high-quality food, you must want to. It is not enough to know how.

⑧ Good understanding of the basics

Experimentation and innovation in cooking are the order of the day. Brilliant chefs are breaking old boundaries, inventing dishes that would have been unthinkable years ago. There seems to be no limit to what can be tried.

However, the very chefs who seem to be most revolutionary are the first to insist on the importance of solid grounding in basic techniques and in the classic methods practiced since Escoffier's day. In order to innovate, you have to know where to begin.

For the beginner, knowing the basics will help you take better advantage of your experience. When you watch a practiced cook at work, you will understand better what you are seeing and will know what questions to ask. In order to play great music on the piano, you first have to learn to play scales and exercises.

Note

- persevere : to try to do or continue doing something in a determined way, despite difficulties
- overcome : to prevail over; surmount
- face : to confront with complete awareness
- career : a chosen pursuit; a profession or occupation
- code : a systematic collection of regulations and rules of procedure or conduct
- rush : general haste or busyness
- keep track : If you keep track, you make certain that you know what is happening or has happened to someone or something.
- split : being divided or separated
- count : to have value or importance; to matter
- dig in : to begin to work intensively
- click : to function well together; hit it off
- in the air : prevalent
- grueling : extremely tiring and difficult, and demanding great effort and determination
- drudgery : hard monotonous routine work
- canapé : an appetizer prepared on a base such as toast or crackers.
- staff : the group of people who work for an organization
- cooperate : work together on a common enterprise or project
- ego : an exaggerated sense of self-importance; conceit
- petty : of small importance; trivial
- jealousy : a feeling of jealous envy (especially of a rival)
- in the way : in a position to obstruct, hinder, or interfere
- temper : the usual state of your feelings which makes you become angry easily or stay calm
- tantrum : a sudden period of uncontrolled childish anger
- inventory : a detailed list of all the items in a place
- deal with : to take action on; to manage
- purveyor : someone who supplies provisions (especially food)

- substitute : one that takes the place of another; a replacement
- get off to : to start to do something in a particular way
- running start : a quick or auspicious beginning
- gourmet : a person who knows a lot about food and cooking, and who enjoys eating high-quality food
- duckling : young duck
- à l'orange : with orange glaze and/or sauce
- grounding : an area of knowledge or experience; a subject
- innovate : to introduce changes and new ideas
- practiced : skillful after much practice
- scale : a set of notes played or sung in order, going up or down
- exercises : Exercises are a ceremony which includes speeches and usually traditional music or activities

References

Algonquin College, "Algonquin College Culinary Laboratory Uniform and Code of Conduct Policy," August 25th, 2016, Retrieved Jan. 10, 2018 from http://www.algonquincollege.com/hospitalityandtourism/news/algonquin-college-culinary-laboratory-uniform-code-conduct-policy-fall-2016/

Ema, Jema, "I am a chef.," Retrieved Jan. 10, 2007 from http://www.globalchefs.com/article/archive/art062iam.htm)

Larousse, David Paul, 1996, The Professional Garde Manger(New York: John Wiley & Sons, Inc.), pp.19~20.

Retrieved Jan. 10, 2004 from
http://www.globalchefs.com/article/archive/art062iam.htm

Retrieved Jan. 13, 2018 from http://dictionary.cambridge.org/

Retrieved Jan. 6, 2018 from http://encarta.msn.com/encnet/features/dictionary/

Retrieved Jan. 5, 2018 from http://www.merriam-webster.com/dictionary/

Retrieved Jan. 5, 2018 from https://www.onelook.com/

Retrieved Jan. 5, 2018 from https://en.oxforddictionaries.com/

Chapter 05

All about Chefs

Description : White House Executive Chef Cristeta Comerford, foreground, briefs staff on preparations for the state dinner honoring Mexico in the State Dining Room of the White House on May 19, 2010.
(Source : Retrieved 26 Jan 2018 from https://commons.wikimedia.org/wiki/File:White_House_Executive_Chef_Cristeta_Comerford_briefing_staff.jpg

"If you want to become a great chef, you have to work with great chefs. And that's exactly what I did."

- Gordon Ramsay (born 8 November 1966), a British celebrity chef, restaurateur, and television personality

1. Definition of a Chef

While most dictionaries define a chef as a skilled, trained and professional cook, typically the chief cook in a restaurant or hotel (Oxford Dictionary; Cambridge English Dictionary; Collins English Dictionary, n.d.), a chef is a person who cooks professionally for other people. Although over time the term has come to describe any person who cooks for a living, traditionally it refers to a highly skilled professional who is proficient in all aspects of food preparation (Wikipedia, n.d.).

2. A true Chef

The term "chef," is considered a mark of respect and distinction that describes a professional cook who has reached the position through hard work and dedication to quality (Foundations of Restaurant Management & Culinary Arts, n.d.). Those chefs who have made, or will make, the most lasting impression on this industry know that their success depends on their ability to fulfill many different roles. A true chef is, among other things, a lifelong student, a teacher, a craftsman, a leader, and a manager. An open and inquiring mind, an appreciation of and dedication to quality and excellence, and a sense of responsibility to self and the community are among the professional chef's cardinal virtues (Donovan, 1996).

3. The Kitchen Brigade

As in all effective organizations, work has been broken down into parts and assigned to smaller units where every member knows his or her place and responsibility. This organizational structure is known as the "Brigade de cuisine", the kitchen brigade, and you will find it almost everywhere in the world (Professionalsecrets, n.d.). The kitchen brigade is an organizational hierarchy for professional kitchens organized by the legendary French chef, Georges Auguste Escoffier.

The idea was to avoid duplication of effort, and to help facilitate communication between the various staff members. The system used a hierarchical organization, with a strict chain of command based on rank (Culinarylore, n.d.).

Almost all professional kitchens embrace this system, the only thing that varies from one workplace to another is the number of stations and chefs, depending on the size of the restaurant. Georges August Escoffier is credited for developing the kitchen brigade, which assigns certain responsibilities to kitchen staff. Figure 5-1 shows you the basic model (Professionalsecrets, n.d.).

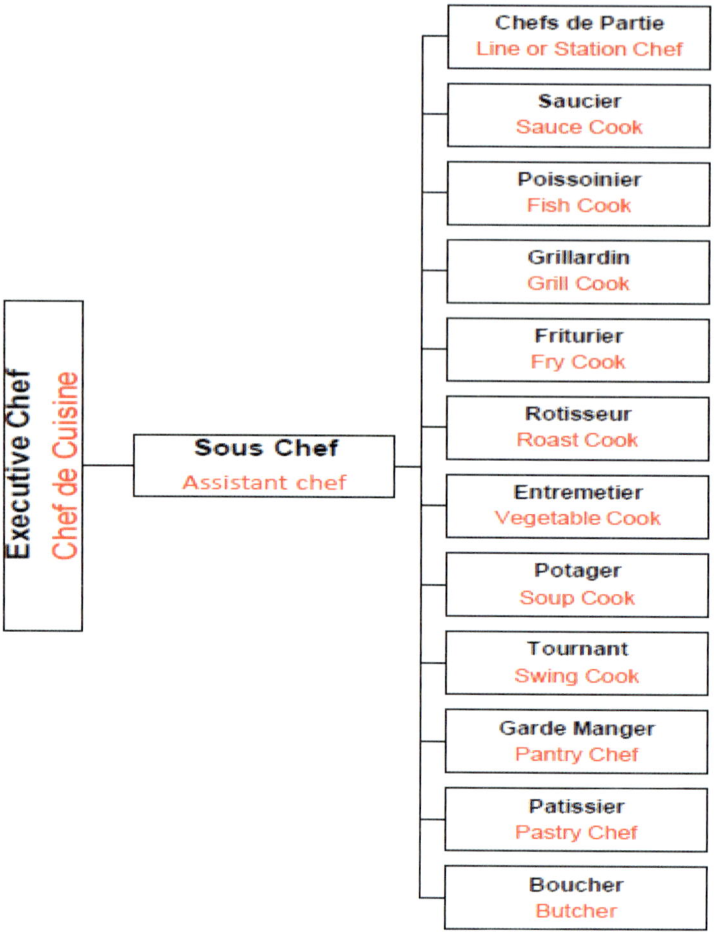

[Figure 5–1] Culinary Kitchen Brigade

(Source : Culinary Kitchen Brigade, Retrieved Jan. 9, 2018 from http://cte.sfasu.edu/wp-content/uploads/2015/05/Culinary-Kitchen-Brigade.pdf)

Chef de cuisine (kitchen chef; literally "chief of kitchen") is responsible for overall management of kitchen; supervises staff, creates menus and new recipes with the assistance of the restaurant manager, makes purchases of raw food items, trains apprentices, and maintains a sanitary and hygienic environment for the preparation of food.

Sous-chef de cuisine (deputy/second kitchen chef; literally "subchief") receives orders directly from the chef de cuisine for the management of the kitchen, and often serves as the representative when the chef de cuisine is not present.

Chef de partie (senior chef; literally "chief of party"; party used here as a group, in the sense of a military detail) is responsible for managing a given station in the kitchen, specializing in preparing particular dishes there. Those who work in a lesser station are commonly referred to as a demi-chef.

Saucier (saucemaker/sauté cook) prepares sauces and warm hors d'oeuvres, completes meat dishes, and in smaller restaurants, may work on fish dishes and prepare sautéed items. This is one of the most respected positions in the kitchen brigade.

Poissonnier (fish cook) prepares fish and seafood dishes.

Grillardin (grill cook) in larger kitchens, prepares grilled foods instead of the rôtisseur.

Friturier (fry cook) in larger kitchens, prepares fried foods instead of the rôtisseur.

Rôtisseur (roast cook) manages a team of cooks that roasts, broils, and deep fries dishes.

Entremetier (entrée preparer) prepares soups and other dishes not involving meat or fish, including vegetable dishes and egg dishes.

Potager (soup cook) in larger kitchens, reports to the entremetier and prepares the soups.

Tournant (spare hand/roundsman) moves throughout the kitchen, assisting other positions in kitchen.

Garde manger (pantry supervisor; literally "food keeper") is responsible for preparation of cold hors d'oeuvres, pâtés, terrines and aspics; prepares salads; organizes large buffet displays; and prepares charcuterie items.

Pâtissier (pastry cook) prepares desserts and other meal-end sweets, and for locations without a boulanger, also prepares breads and other baked items; may also prepare pasta for the restaurant.

Boucher (butcher) butchers meats, poultry, and sometimes fish; may also be in charge of breading meat and fish items.

4. Difference between a Cook and a Chef

Consider the difference between a cook and a chef. Cooks and chefs are similar culinary occupations that differ mainly by seniority and skill levels (Study, n.d.). Dr. Nordstrom always emphasizes in his seminars the difference between a cook and a chef: the cook follows recipes whereas the chef understands principles and applies them (Lemke, 2009).

These two jobs are sometimes thought of as one in the same, probably due to the fact that a chef is technically a cook, but just a more skilled one who's in charge. While both prepare food, a chef has the final say in the kitchen. Chefs lead a team of cooks, whose duties vary by the establishment where they work. Without proper supervision from the chef, the whole process could lag, thus one must be able to coordinate a crew. Aside from cooking and giving direction, a chef creates menus and recipes, which cooks must follow to the letter. Both cooks and chefs hone their skills through training and experience, and their jobs are often demanding, fast-paced, and somewhat hazardous (Study.com, n.d.). In terms of job responsibility, Table 5-1 shows you job responsibilities of a cook and a chef.

Table 5-1 Job responsibilities of a cook and a chef

Job responsibilities of a cook	Job responsibilities of a chef
• Storing and gathering ingredients • Cleaning their work stations • Handling various kitchen appliances • Following recipes and carrying out customer orders • Preparing, heating, and arranging food	• Training and hiring crew members • Inspecting food for freshness and sanitation • Ordering and maintaining the inventory of food and supplies • Promoting their business • Addressing customers' concerns

(Source : Study.com, "Difference Between Cook & Chef," Retrieved 9 Jan 2018 from https://study.com/articles/difference_between_cook_chef.html

5. Stage

Staging is an unpaid internship when a cook or chef works briefly, for free, in another chef's kitchen to learn and be exposed to new techniques and cuisines. The term originates from the French word stagiaire meaning trainee, apprentice or intern. The French term commis is often used interchangeably with the aforementioned terms (Wikipedia, 2018).

This can apply to inexperienced cooks, or to experienced professionals who want to learn new cuisines. Ferran Adria's El Bulli was flooded with applications from aspiring stagiaires, for instance, all of whom were at the top of their fields in their home countries (Crystal, 2014).

Note

- profession : a type of job that needs special training or skill, especially one that needs a high level of education
- dedication : the hard work and effort that sb puts into an activity or purpose because they think it is important: hard work and dedication
- craftsman : a skilled person, especially one who makes beautiful things by hand
- appreciation : a full or sympathetic understanding of sth, such as a situation or a problem, and of what it involves
- community : all the people who live in a particular area, country, etc. when talked about as a group
- cardinal : most important; having other things based on it
- virtue : a particular good quality or habit
- brigade : a group of people organized for special activity
- detail : a group of soldiers or police officers given a particular job
- boulanger (baker) : In larger restaurants prepares bread, cakes, and breakfast pastries instead of the pâtissier.
- hierarchy : a system in which people or things are arranged according to their importance
- legendary : very famous or well known for a long time
- embrace : to accept and include something
- credit : to believe that something is true
- seniority : greater age, or a more important social position

6. Food Preparation Workers

Food preparation workers perform many routine tasks under the direction of cooks, chefs, or food service managers. Food preparation workers prepare cold foods, slice meat, peel and cut vegetables, brew coffee or tea, and perform many other food service tasks (Bls, n.d.).

7. Culinarians

A dictionary definition of a culinarian is a person skilled in the preparation of food (Thefreedictionary, n.d.). ACF defines a culinarian as a person who is positioned in any one station in a food service operation, responsible for preparing and cooking sauces, cold foods, fish, soups and stocks, meats, vegetables, eggs and other food items (Acfchefs, 2009).

If you're interested in a career as a chef, you need to know about the Culinarian Code. The Culinarian Code offers guidelines for chefs to work ethically, in ways that honor the profession and that uplift other chefs. Understanding the Culinarian Code is essential for prospective chefs (Ecpi, n.d.). Below is the American Culinary Federation's Culinarian's Code which was adopted at the Board of Governors, August 3, 2010 (See Table 5-2; Acfchefs, 2010). Let's look at it!

Table 5-2 Culinarian's Code

"As a proud member of the American Culinary Federation,
I pledge to share my professional knowledge and skill with all culinarians.
I will place honor, fairness, cooperation and consideration first when dealing with my colleagues.
I will keep all comments professional and respectful when dealing with my colleagues.
I will protect all members from the use of unfair means, unnecessary risks and unethical behavior when used against them for another's personal gain.
I will support the success, growth, and future of my colleagues and this great federation."

Source: Acf, "culinarian's code," Retrieved 8 Jan 2018 from https://www.acfchefs.org/download/documents/apprenticeship/culinarians_code.pdf

8. Culinary Artists

A culinary artist is not responsible for making any painting or doing any performances but the person is responsible for making meals. A culinary artist can work either for recreation or as a professional (Collegeinfo, n.d.; Altiusdirectory, n.d.). A culinary artist is someone educated in the preparation of food for restaurants. As a professional, he is more commonly referred to as a chef or head cook. Some achieve this level with a diploma and hands-on training, but many chefs complete two- or four-year culinary programs.

The informal label "culinary artist" depicts the way passionate chefs see themselves. They consider themselves artists of food preparation much in the same way a painter paints and a musician composes and plays music. This enthusiasm for the work and the process of cooking helps top chefs overcome the stress of their jobs. Along with their love for cooking, many also enjoy the restaurant atmosphere and the kitchen environment (Kokemuller, n.d.).

9. Other Chef-related Titles

1) Celebrity chef

A celebrity chef is a kitchen chef who has become famous and well known. Today celebrity chefs often become celebrities by presenting cookery advice and demonstrations via mass media, especially television. Several chefs have been credited with being the first celebrity chef, among them historically Bartolomeo Scappi and Marie-Antoine Carême.

In the modern era since the advent of television several chefs have been attributed the title of the "first celebrity chef", including Julia Child in the United States and Fanny Cradock in the UK. While television is ultimately the primary way for a chef to become a celebrity, some have achieved this through success in the kitchen, publications and achieving such awards as Michelin stars while others are home cooks (Wikipedia, 2018).

Similarly, In South Korea, a celebrity chef is referred to as a Cheftainer which is a combination of the words chef and entertainer (Korea Times, 2015; Sohn, 2015).

2) Master chef

MasterChef is a competitive cooking show television format created by Franc Roddam, which originated with the UK version in July 1990. The format was revived and updated for the BBC in February 2005 by executive producers Roddam and John Silver and series producer Karen Ross. In 2009, the format was re-developed in Australia where it was transformed into the current iteration of the programme. This gave the programme a new dynamic.

The show's format has been exported around the world under the same MasterChef logo, and is now produced in more than 40 countries and airs in over 200 territories (Wikipedia, 2018).

The title of Certified Master Chef (CMC), presented solely by the American Culinary Federation (ACF) in the U.S., is the highest level of certification a chef can receive. It represents the pinnacle of professionalism and skill. Today, there are 68 CMCs and 10 Certified Master Pastry Chefs® (CMPC) in the nation (Acfchefs, 2017).

To apply for the CMC exam, a candidate must be a Certified Executive Chef® or Certified Culinary Educator®, provide two letters of recommendation from current CMCs or CMPCs, and have completed education courses on sanitation and food safety, cost management, management and wine. The candidate must also secure funding for the cost of the exam process including the exam fee, travel expenses and practice materials.

During the eight-day exam, candidates must maintain an average score of 75 out of 100 points to be eligible to continue. Scores are tallied based on kitchen skills, plate presentation and taste. Candidates are tested on the following eight subjects by ACF-certified chefs: Healthy cooking, Buffet catering, Classical cuisine, Freestyle cooking, Global cuisine, Baking and pastry, Continental and Northern Europe cuisines, and Market basket.

On the other hand, this title is called as "Master Craftsman Cook," or 기능장 in Korean whose certification is given out to those chefs who have exceeded a certain level after a test of 60 multiple choice questions on culinary knowledge and 5-hour test of culinary skills (Human Resources Development Service of Korea, n.d.).

Description : Logo & Wordmark of MasterChef Australia(L). Logo of the Spanish gastronomy competition MasterChef Junior(R)

(Source : Retrieved 30 Jan 2018 from
https://commons.wikimedia.org/wiki/File:MasterChef_Australia_Logo_%26_Wordmark.svg
https://commons.wikimedia.org/wiki/File:Masterchef-junior-logo.jpg)

3) Top chef

Top Chef is an American reality competition television series which premiered on March 8, 2006, on Bravo. The show features chefs competing against each other in various culinary challenges. They are judged by a panel of professional chefs and other notables from the food and wine industry with one or more contestants eliminated in each episode. The show is produced by Magical Elves Productions, the same company that created Project Runway.

On January 24, 2017, Bravo announced that it had renewed Top Chef for a fifteenth season. The new season was filmed in Colorado, with challenges set in Denver, Boulder, Telluride, and Aspen, and premiered on December 7, 2017 (Wikipedia, 2018).

Description : The finalist studio of the 6th edition of the Top Chef Polska program organized in Hala Mera in Warsaw less than an hour before the start of the show.

(Source : Retrieved 30 Jan 2018 from https://commons.wikimedia.org/w/index.php?search=Top+chef&title=Special:Search&go=Go&searchToken=btqi1v4n50x8c7ajwy2v6apzq#/media/File:Top_Chef_Polska_-_fina%C5%82_6._edycji,_Hala_Mera,_2016-05-04.jpg)

4) Iron chef

Iron Chef (料理の鉄人 Ryōri no Tetsujin, literally "Ironmen of Cooking") is a Japanese television cooking show produced by Fuji Television. The series, which premiered on October 10, 1993, is a stylized cook-off featuring guest chefs challenging one of the show's resident "Iron Chefs" in a timed cooking battle built around a specific theme ingredient. The series ended on September 24, 1999, although occasional specials were produced until 2002. The series aired 309 episodes. Repeats are regularly aired on the Food Network in Canada, the Cooking Channel in the United States and on Special Broadcasting Service in Australia. Fuji TV aired a new version of the show, titled Iron Chef (アイアンシェフ Aian Shefu), starting on October 26, 2012 (Wikipedia, 2018).

Description : Members of the 509th Force Support Squadron pose for a photo prior to the Global Strike Iron Chef Challenge at Whiteman Air Force Base, Mo., Sept. 4, 2015.

(Source : Retrieved 30 Jan 2018 from http://www.whiteman.af.mil/News/Article-Display/Article/835917/the-heat-is-on-whiteman-fss-teams-compete-in-iron-chef-challenge/)

Note

- uplift : to make someone feel happier or more hopeful
- Board of Governors : 이사회
- depict : to represent or show something in a picture or story
- cookery : the skill or activity of preparing and cooking food
- Bartolomeo Scappi (c. 1500 – 13 April 1577) : He was a famous Italian Renaissance chef.
- Marie-Antoine Carême (8 June 1784 – 12 January 1833) : He was a French chef and an early practitioner and exponent of the elaborate style of cooking known as grande cuisine.
- attribute : to decide as to where something belongs in a scheme
- Julia Child : Julia Carolyn Child (née McWilliams; August 15, 1912 – August 13, 2004) was an American chef, author and television personality. She is recognized for bringing French cuisine to the American public with her debut cookbook, Mastering the Art of French Cooking, and her subsequent television programs, the most notable of which was The French Chef, which premiered in 1963.
- Fanny Cradock : Phyllis Nan Sortain Pechey (26 February 1909 – 27 December 1994), better known as Fanny Cradock, was an English restaurant critic, television celebrity chef and writer frequently appearing on television, at cookery demonstrations and in print with Major Johnnie Cradock who played the part of a slightly bumbling hen-pecked husband.
- pinnacle : the most successful or exciting part of someone's life
- tally : to match or agree with something else
- iteration : the process of doing something again and again, usually to improve it, or one of the times you do it
- premiere : be performed for the first time
- Bravo : (U.S. TV network), an American cable television network
- Magical Elves Productions : Since its formation in 2001, Magical Elves has been one of the most well-respected and successful unscripted production companies in the business.
- Project Runway : Project Runway is an American reality television (TV) series that focuses on fashion design.

References

Acfchefs, "2017 Certified Master Chefs® Exam," Retrieved 8 Jan 2018 from http://www.acfchefs.org/ACF/Certify/Levels/CMC/2017CMCExam/ACF/Certify/Levels/CMC/2017/

Acf, "culinarian's code," Retrieved 8 Jan 2018 from https://www.acfchefs.org/download/documents/apprenticeship/culinarians_code.pdf

Altiusdirectory, "CULINARY ARTS," Retrieved Jan. 13, 2010 from http://www.altiusdirectory.com/Arts/culinary-arts.html

Bls, "Food Preparation Workers," Retrieved 9 Jan 2018 from https://www.bls.gov/ooh/food-preparation-and-serving/food-preparation-workers.htm

Culinarylore, "What Is The Kitchen Brigade?" Retrieved 7 Jan 2018 from http://www.culinarylore.com/food-history:what-is-the-kitchen-brigade

Collegeinfo, "Cooking Up A Career: The Culinary Arts," Retrieved Jan. 13, 2010 from http://www.collegeinfo.com/cooking-up-a-career-the-culinary-arts

Crystal.kitchen, "How to Stage/Intern/Trail at a Restaurant: The Wrong Way," September 17, 2014, Retrieved 26 Jan 2018 from http://www.crystal.kitchen/2014/09/17/how-to-stageinterntrail-at-a-restaurant-the-wrong-way/

Donovan, Mary Deirdew(ed.), 1996, The New Proefessional Chef, 6th ed.(New York:John Wiley & Sons, Inc.), p.11. pp.42～43.

Ecpi, "What Does the Culinarian Code Mean?" Retrieved 19 Jan 2018 from https://www.ecpi.edu/blog/what-does-the-culinarian-code-mean

Foundations of Restaurant Management & Culinary Arts, Retrieved 19 Jan 2018from http://wps.prenhall.com/chet_nra_foundations_1/154/39652/10151014.cw/index.html

Human Resources Development Service of Korea, "국가자격종목별상세정보," Retrieved 19 Jan 2010 from http://www.q-net.or.kr/

Kokemuller, Neil, "Advantages and Disadvanages of Being a Culinary Artist," Retrieved 19 Jan 2018 from http://work.chron.com/advantages-disadvanages-being-culinary-artist-6882.html

Korea Times, "'Cheftainer' cooks up a storm in new TV show". 11 June 2015. Retrieved 19 Jan 2018 from http://www.koreatimes.co.kr/www/news/nation/2015/05/116_179174.html

Lemke, Ljuba, 2009, "ALF (Advanced Lightwire Functionals), Cranial Osteopathy, and Overall Health, Holistic," Health Source, April, Retrieved Jan. 14, 2010 from http://www.alforthodontics.com/ALF_CO_Health.pdf

Professionalsecrets, "Brigade de cuisine – the kitchen brigade," Retrieved 5 Jan 2018 from http://www.professionalsecrets.com/en/ps/ps-university/kitchen-brigade/

Sohn, Ji-young, (17 March 2015). "New generation of cooking shows eyes lone living". The Korea Herald. Retrieved 19 Jan 2018 from http://www.koreaherald.com/view.php?ud=20150317001164

Study.com, "Difference Between Cook & Chef," Retrieved 9 Jan 2018 from https://study.com/articles/difference_between_cook_chef.html

Thefreedictionary, "culinarian," Retrieved Jan. 14, 2010 from http://www.thefreedictionary.com/Culinarian

Retrieved 9 Jan 2018 from https://en.wikipedia.org/wiki/Iron_Chef

Retrieved 9 Jan 2018 from https://en.wikipedia.org/wiki/Top_Chef

Retrieved 26 Jan 2018 from https://en.wikipedia.org/wiki/Stage_(cooking)

Retrieved Jan. 8, 2018 from http://www.answers.com/topic/craft

Retrieved Jan. 9, 2018 from http://en.wiktionary.org/,

Retrieved Jan. 9, 2018 from https://www.collinsdictionary.com/dictionary/english

Retrieved Jan. 9, 2018 from https://dictionary.cambridge.org/

Retrieved Jan. 9, 2018 from https://www.oxforddictionaries.com/

Chapter 06

Michelin Guide: The Last Word in Gourmet Dining

Description : One of the courses in Vertig'O, Michelin star restaurant in Geneva, Switzerland

(Source : Retrieved 26 Jan 2018 from https://commons.wikimedia.org/wiki/File:Carte_Printemps_Spring_menu_Switzerland_Michelin_starred_restaurant.jpg)

"The kitchen really is the castle itself. This is where we spend our happiest moments and where we find the joy of being a family."

- Mario Batali (born September 19, 1960), an American chef, writer, restaurateur, and media personality

1. What is Michelin Guide?

1) History of Michelin Guide

In 1900, the Michelin brothers (Founders of Michelin Tire Company) published the first edition of a guide to France to help drivers maintain their cars, find decent lodging, and eat well while touring. It included addresses of gasoline distributors, garages, tire stockists, public toilets, etc. The guide was distributed free until 1920. In 1926, the guide introduced one star to denote good cooking; two and three stars were added in the early 1930s. The cover of the guide was originally blue, but since 1931 has been red. The first guides for cities outside of Europe were published in 2006 for New York City and in 2007 for San Francisco (Indianwineacademy, n.d.).

During the rest of 20th century, thanks to its serious and unique approach, the Michelin Guides became best-sellers without equals: the guide now rates over 30,000 establishments in over 30 territories across three continents, and more than 30 million Michelin Guides have been sold worldwide since (Guide.michelin, 2017).

2) Stars and Covers

The Michelin Guide conveys its restaurant reviews through two to three-line short summaries and an extensive system of symbols, the most revered of which are its globally renowned stars. Restaurants may receive zero to 3 stars for the quality of their food based on five assessment criteria (See Figure 6-1; Table 6-1; Guide.michelin, 2017).

▌Table 6-1▐ Five assessment criteria

1. Quality of the products
2. Mastery of flavor and cooking techniques
3. The personality of the chef in his cuisine
4. Value for money
5. Consistency between visits

(Source : Guide.michelin, "To the Stars and Beyond, "15 Oct 2017,Retrieved 10 Jan 2018 from https://guide.michelin.com/us/chicago/the-inspection-process)

[Figure 6-1] Michelin Stars Rating Sysrem
(Source : Retrieved 10 Jan 2018 from https://warosu.org/ck/image/wX7T2n6IXZnITMuAp0yE6g)

Restaurant inspectors do not look at the interior decor, table setting, or service quality when awarding stars—these are instead indicated by the number of 'covers' it receives, represented by the fork and spoon symbol (See Figure 6-2; Guide.michelin, 2017). Rankings range from one to five: One fork and spoon represents a "comfortable restaurant" and five signifies a "luxurious restaurant". Forks and spoons colored red designate a restaurant that is considered "pleasant" as well (Wikipedia, 2018).

[Figure 6-2] Fork and spoon ratings
(Source : Guide.michelin, "To the Stars and Beyond, "15 Oct 2017, Retrieved 10 Jan 2018 from https://guide.michelin.com/us/chicago/the-inspection-process)

An establishment with three stars can offer exceptional cuisine worth a special journey. Michelin's three-star rating, coveted by chefs and restaurateurs, is rare with 120 establishments around the world holding that distinction. Even though very few restaurants manage to make it into three-star territory, Japan has 34 of them, the highest number in the world according to the 2018 Michelin Guide (Wikipedia, 2018). Statistics of Table 6-2 shows countries by number of 3-star restaurants in November 2018.

Table 6-2 List of Michelin 3-star restaurants by country (as of 2017)

Name of nation	Number of restaurant	Remarks
Belgium	2	
China	10	Shanghai(2), Hong Kong(6), Macau(2)
Denmark	1	
France	27	
Germany	11	
Italy	9	
Japan	34	
Monaco	1	
Netherlands	3	
Norway	1	
Singapore	1	
South Korea	2	
Spain	11	
Switzerland	3	
United Kingdom	5	
United States	13	

(Source : Retrieved Jan. 19, 2018 from ttps://en.wikipedia.org/wiki/List_of_Michelin_3-star_restaurants)

3) Bib Gourmand and The Plate Michelin

Since 1955, the guide has also highlighted restaurants offering "exceptionally good food at moderate prices", a feature now called "Bib Gourmand". Bib (Bibendum) is the company's nickname for the Michelin Man, its corporate logo for over a century.

They must offer menu items priced below a maximum determined by local economic standards (Wikipedia, 2017). Namely, a three-course meal with starter, main course and dessert, within a fixed price range (which today stands at €36 in most European cities, US$40 in American cities, HK300 in Hong Kong, Y5,000 in Tokyo and KRW35,000 in Seoul (See Figure 6-3; Guide.michelin, 2017).

[Figure 6-3] Michelin Bib Gourmand logo
(Source : Retrieved 10 Jan 2018 from http://eszcajg.blog.hu/)

In the latest 2016 edition of the Paris guide, a brand new L'assiette or The Plate symbol was launched to recognize restaurants that 'simply serve good food' (See Figure 6-4; Guide.michelin, 2017).

[Figure 6-4] The Michelin Plate symbol
(Source : Retrieved 10 Jan 2018 from http://descargasgratis.us/compsupport.us/20170422_decoration-de-table-theme-cuisine-12/)

4) The Inspection Process

Who are the Michelin Guide's restaurant inspectors and how do they go about doing their jobs? Envied by many for having quite possibly the best job in the world, the Michelin Guide's stable of inspectors are all full-time employees of the Michelin Group who dine out regularly to put forth the best consumer recommendations for hotels and restaurant experiences (Guide.michelin,com, 2017).

Most of the them have studied in the best hospitality schools in the world, are widely travelled and have lived and worked in various countries around the world — and are collectively responsible for rating more than 30,000 hotels and restaurants in over 30 countries across three continents. The inspector travels 30,000 km a year on average, eats some 250 meals in restaurants and sleeps in more than 160 hotels in order to select the best restaurants and hotels in all comfort and price categories. Working anonymously, the inspector is an ordinary customers who books a table in restaurants, orders, dines, never takes notes during meals and pays his or her own bill (Guide.michelin,co.kr, n.d.).

This anonymity is what makes the Michelin Guide so successful. Inspectors don't want to be treated differently from anyone else. In their plate, they have exactly what other customers are served. Nothing more, nothing less. It is only after paying their bill that inspectors may introduce themselves and ask for more information, if necessary (Guide.michelin,co.kr, n.d.).

To maintain the independence of their opinion, the inspectors always dine out anonymously, pay for their meals, and subsequently rate their experience according to five publicly acknowledged assessment criteria (See Table 6-1; Guide.michelin,com, 2017). These objective criteria are respected by all Michelin guide inspectors, whether in Japan, the United States, China or Europe. Used around the world, the criteria guarantee a consistent selection. A one-star restaurant delivers the same value regardless of whether it is located in Paris, New York or Tokyo (Guide.michelin,co.kr, n.d.).

Food trends and dining technologies may have come and gone, but for over a century, the Michelin Guide has held firm to its founding mission of fostering a culture of travel and eating out, and its promise of helping people make the right choice, based on six core values (See Table 6-3; Guide.michelin,com, n.d.).

Table 6-3 Six core values

Anonymity	Although our "inspectors" work for the Michelin guide, they are above all customers like any other, testing restaurants in complete anonymity in order to ensure that they do not receive any special treatment.
Independence	All our inspectors are employees of the Michelin group, who always pay for their meals in the restaurants they are testing to ensure that they do not receive any special treatment.
Expertise	Our inspectors are also real experts in the catering and hospitality industries, sectors in which many of them have previously worked.
Reliability	The different categories awarded by the guide are never just the result of one person's judgement; they are formed by a collective decision which is the result of a long process.
Passion	What would be the point of so much work and such a strict approach if our inspectors did not enjoy eating?
Quality	Any restaurant can be recommended by our guide as long as its food is of high quality.

(Source : Guide.michelin,, "Inspection processes," Retrieved 10 Jan 2018 from https://guide.michelin.co.kr/en/about/inspection-processes/)

5) Non-restaurant food

With the blurring of lines between restaurants and other eateries, Michelin is adapting too. From 2014, it had a separate listing for gastropubs in Ireland. The 2016 Guide for Hong Kong and Macau introduced an overview of notable street food establishments. The Singapore guide that year introduced the first Michelin stars for street food locations, for Hong Kong Soya Sauce Chicken Rice and Noodle and Hill Street Tai Hwa Pork Noodle (Wikipedia, 2018).

Description : Exterior view of The Hand and Flowers

(Source : Retrieved 29 Jan 2018 from
https://www.tripsavvy.com/the-hand-and-flowers-restaurant-review-1662489)

Description : Hong Kong Soya Sauce Chicken Rice and Noodle is a street food stall in Singapore.(L), Bak chor mee at Hill Street Tai Hwa Pork Noodle in Singapore.(R)

(Source : Retrieved 29 Jan 2018 from
https://en.wikipedia.org/wiki/Hong_Kong_Soya_Sauce_Chicken_Rice_and_Noodle#/media/File:Hong_Kong_Soya_Sauce_Chicken_Rice_and_Noodle_-_Singapore_-_March_28_2017.jpg
https://commons.wikimedia.org/wiki/File:Bak-chor-mee.jpg

2. The Michelin Guide Seoul

1) The first edition of the Michelin Guide Seoul 2017

Michelin today unveiled the very first selection for the Michelin Guide Seoul 2017, reflecting both the diversity of the culinary offerings in the city and its gastronomic dynamism. Gaon and la Yeon obtain three stars in the very first Michelin guide Seoul selection (Michelin, 2017)!

The richness of this first selection is the sign that today Seoul has emerged as a mecca of world gastronomy. The quality, the potential of the culinary offerings as well as the eclectic cuisine that can be found there delighted our inspectors, who discovered some exceptional restaurants in Seoul. The cuisine at La Yeon led by chef Kim Sung Il immerses diners in a true gastronomic experience. The sophistication of the dishes combined with the contemporary approach the chef gives to Korean tradition lifts this restaurant to the level of experiences that are worth the trip.

Three restaurants obtained two stars in this first selection in Seoul: Gotgan, an establishment that impresses both with the panoramic view it offers of the city and the sophistication of the Korean cuisine offered by chef LEE — cuisine in which 30 year old soy sauce or soybean paste replaces traditional seasonings. Kwon Sook Soo, whose name was inspired by "sooksoo" an ancient Korean word meaning "professional chef", also received two stars. Chef Kwon WOO JOONG infuses modern touches into traditional Korean food by in particular associating unusual seasonal products with the most common ingredients to create original and unconventional flavours.

Finally, the restaurant Pierre Gagnaire was awarded two stars. The eponymous restaurant of the famous French chef Pierre GAGNAIRE, who thereby totals 16 stars worldwide, offers French cuisine reflecting the creative style of the Parisian chef while being based on local ingredients.

The Michelin Guide Seoul 2017 also gave nineteen restaurants one star: establishments that reflect the great diversity and richness of the gastronomy available in Seoul, be it traditional Korean food as offered by Poom or Hamo or more contemporary as in Twenty Four Seasons or Jungsik; Italian as in Ristorente Eo, French as in L'Amitié and Votre Maison, or sushi specialities in Kojima.

The full selection in the Michelin Guide Seoul 2017 is available on the website www.guide.michelin.co.kr. This selection includes:

- 2 restaurants with three stars
- 3 restaurants with two stars
- 19 restaurants with one star

2) The second edition of the Michelin Guide Seoul 2018

Michelin today unveiled the second edition of the Michelin Guide Seoul 2018, which features a total of 175 restaurants in the city (Michelin, 2018).

"We are excited to announce that our selection has been enriched by newly found restaurants, showcasing the vibrancy of the local dining scene in Seoul" comments Michael ELLIS, International Director in charge of the Michelin guides.

In this new selection, the restaurants Ga On and La Yeon are awarded three stars, a distinction gained last year in the very first edition of the Michelin guide Seoul.

Two restaurants are newly awarded two stars:Jungsik, where the renowned Chef Yim Jung-sik, with his Seoul flagship and New York restaurants—is credited with introducing Korean cuisine to the world with an innovative flair that is entirely his own. Drawing inspiration from the familiar—kimbap, bibimbap, gujeolpan and bossam—he creates something unexpected yet surprisingly evocative and authentic in his cuisine. Also awarded two stars, the sophisticated restaurant Kojima-Sushi offers some of the most exquisite Japanese food in Seoul. The cuisine offered the chef's technical skill as well as his mastery of the art of sushi.

The Michelin guide Seoul 2018 lists a total of 18 one-starred restaurants, of which 4 are new.

Exquisine, a restaurant where Chef Jang Kyung-won's creativity is driven by his knowledge of local ingredients and understanding the balance between each component that leads to flavors that ultimately reflect his unique signature. The restaurant offers a fixed menu for lunch and dinner that change frequently depending on the availability of ingredients. The fresh herbs are from the restaurant's garden.

Dosa also gains one star: Chef Back Seung-wook serves creative and modern cuisine that pays homage to his Korean roots. The open kitchen, which offers a dynamic view of the chefs in action, makes the dining experience here that much more enjoyable.

Joo Ok, a Korean-style bistro by Chef Shin Chang-ho, who built his career at Nobu Miami, is awarded one star. His inventive interpretations of food ingredients, together with his exquisite arrangements on the plate, are a delight to experience.

Lastly, Table for Four earns its first star. Chef Kim Sung Woon serves European cuisine and changes the menu based on the seafood that's in season, with a wonderful presentation.

48 restaurants are awarded Bib Gourmand in the new selection of the Michelin guide Seoul 2018. Among them, 17 are newly awarded, each reflecting the diversity of the local cuisine that the inspectors discovered by wandering the streets of Seoul. Bib Gourmand distinction is given by the inspectors to establishments offering a quality menu for a maximum of 35,000 KRW.

The full selection in the Michelin Guide Seoul 2018 is available on the website www.guide.michelin.co.kr.

This selection includes:

- 2 restaurants with three stars
- 4 restaurants with two stars, of which 2 are new
- 18 restaurants with one star, of which 4 are new
- 48 restaurants with Bib Gourmand, of which 17 are new

Note

- the last word (in something) : (~의) 첨단
- vibrancy : the quality or state of being vibrant
- decent : socially acceptable or good
- stockist : a shop that sells a particular type of goods
- covers : (식탁 위의) 한 사람분의 식기
- put forth : to present; propose
- hold firm (to something) : (~을) 단단히 지키다(고수하다)
- gastropub : a pub that serves good quality food
- eclectic : composed of elements drawn from various sources
- evocative : vivid and seemingly realistic as in the artistic representation of a particular time, place, etc.
- accolade : an honor given to someone for their work

References

Guide.michelin, "To the Stars and Beyond," 15 Oct 2017, Retrieved 10 Jan 2018 from https://guide.michelin.com/us/chicago/the-inspection-process

Guide.michelin, "About Us," 12 Oct 2017, Retrieved 10 Jan 2018 from https://guide.michelin.com/us/chicago/about-us

Guide.michelin, "The Inspection Process," 12 Oct 2017, Retrieved 10 Jan 2018 from https://guide.michelin.com/us/chicago/the-inspection-process

Indianwineacademy, "Fine Dining Feature: Michelin Guide to debut in Japan," Retrieved 10 Jan 2018 from http://www.indianwineacademy.com/dm_116_item_2.asp

Michelin, "The MICHELIN Guide Seoul 2017 selection reflects the eclecticism and the potential of the gastronomic scene in the city," 11/07/2016, Retrieved 10 Jan 2018 from https://www.michelin.com/eng/media-room/press-and-news/press-releases/Products-Services/The-MICHELIN-Guide-Seoul-2017-selection-reflects-the-eclecticism-and-the-potential-of-the-gastronomic-scene-in-the-city

Michelin, "Guide MICHELIN - Seoul 2018 - Jungsik and Kojima-Sushi obtain twostars in the 2nd edition of the guide," 11/08/2017, Retrieved 10 Jan 2018 from https://www.michelin.com/eng/media-room/press-and-news/press-releases/Products-Services/Guide-MICHELIN-Seoul-2018-Jungsik-and-Kojima-Sushi-obtain-two-stars-in-the-2nd-edition-of-the-guide

Retrieved 26 Jan 2018 from https://commons.wikimedia.org/wiki/File:Carte_Printemps_Spring_menu_Switzerland_Michelin_starred_restaurant.jpg)

Retrieved 3 Jan 2018 from http://descargasgratis.us/compsupport.us/20170422_decoration-de-table-theme-cuisine-12/

Retrieved 3 Jan 2018 from https://www.michelin.com/fre/innovation/domaines-d-intervention/innovation-mobilite/1900-Premier-Guide-Michelin

Retrieved 3 Jan 2018 from http://eszcajg.blog.hu/

Retrieved 3 Jan 2018 from https://warosu.org/ck/image/wX7T2n6IXZnITMuAp0yE6g

Retrieved 3 Jan 2018 from https://en.wikipedia.org/wiki/Michelin_Guide

Retrieved Jan 4, 2018 from http://www.answers.com/topic/craft

Retrieved Jan 4, 2018 from http://en.wiktionary.org/

Retrieved Jan 4, 2018 from https://www.collinsdictionary.com/dictionary/english

Retrieved Jan 4, 2018 from https://dictionary.cambridge.org/

Retrieved Jan 4, 2018 from https://www.oxforddictionaries.com/

Chapter 07

Essential Culinary Terms & New Phenomena and Concepts

(Source : A restaurant placard, Santorini, Greece(Source : Retrieved 5 Jan 2018 from https://en.wikipedia.org/wiki/Slow_Food#/media/File:SlowFoodThera06676.JPG)

"Show me your garden and I shall tell you what you are."

- Alfred Austin (30 May 1835 - 2 June 1913), an English poet

1. Essential Culinary Terms

1) Haute cuisine vs Nouvelle cuisine

Haute cuisine (French: literally "high cooking") or Grande cuisine refers to the cuisine of "high level" establishments, gourmet restaurants and luxury hotels. Haute cuisine is characterized by meticulous preparation and careful presentation of food, at a high price level (Wikipedia, 2017).

Nouvelle cuisine (French, "new cuisine") is an approach to cooking and food presentation in French cuisine. In contrast to cuisine classique, an older form of haute cuisine, nouvelle cuisine is characterized by lighter, more delicate dishes and an increased emphasis on presentation. It was popularized in the 1960s by the food critics Henri Gault, who invented the phrase, and his colleagues André Gayot and Christian Millau in a new restaurant guide, the Gault-Millau, or Le Nouveau Guide (Wikipedia, 2017).

2) French paradox

The French paradox is a catchphrase, first used in the late 1980s, that summarizes the apparently paradoxical epidemiological observation that French people have a relatively low incidence of coronary heart disease (CHD), while having a diet relatively rich in saturated fats, in apparent contradiction to the widely held belief that the high consumption of such fats is a risk factor for CHD. The paradox is that if the thesis linking saturated fats to CHD is valid, the French ought to have a higher rate of CHD than comparable countries where the per capita consumption of such fats is lower (Wikipedia, 2017).

Description : Brie de Meaux (cow's milk cheese)

(Source : Retrieved 27 Jan 2018 from https://commons.wikimedia.org/wiki/File:Brie_01.jpg)

3) Macrobiotic diet

A macrobiotic diet (or macrobiotics) is a fad diet fixed on ideas about types of food drawn from Zen Buddhism. The diet attempts to balance the supposed yin and yang elements of food and cookware. Major principles of macrobiotic diets are to reduce animal product, eat locally grown foods that are in season, and consume meals in moderation (Wikipedia, 2017).

Description : Picture with some basic macrobiotic ingredients: (from left to right, 1st line) tofu, wheat miso, bancha tea, umeboshi prumes (from left to right, 2nd line) brown rice, sea salt, nori

(Source : Retrieved 27 Jan 2018 from https://commons.wikimedia.org/wiki/File:Some_Basic_Macrobiotic_Ingredients.JPG)

4) Yin-Yang Foods according to Macrobiotic diet

In Chinese philosophy and religion there are two principles, one is Yin and the other is Yang. Yin represents negative, dark and female or feminine. Yang represents positive, bright and masculine.

In Chinese cooking, when chefs design or think of an idea for a dish and menu they will try to find the "perfect balance" of the food. Another thing about Yin and Yang in Chinese cooking is the cooking methods. Generally Chinese people think the Yin cooking methods are boiling, poaching and steaming. The Yang methods are deep-frying, roasting and stir-frying.

In China and Taiwan, most people don't use "Yin and Yang" to describe food but instead use "Hot and Cold". The hot and cold here doesn't relate to the temperature but the attributes of the food (See Table 7-1; Wan, 2017).

Table 7-1 List of Yin and Yang foods

Yin (cold) foods
Mung beans, bean curd and sprouts, all bland or boiled foods, the cabbage family, carrots and celery, cucumber, banana, duck, coconut, black berry, crabs and clams. American ginseng, most greens, honey, melons, milk, pears, pork, potatoes, seaweed and soybean products, white turnips, water and watercress, winter squash, most white foods.
Yang (hot) foods
Bamboo, beef, duck, broiled meats, catfish, chicken and chicken soup, eggs and eggplant, papaya and pumpkin mango, cherry, fatty meats and fried foods, garlic and ginger, Korean ginseng, glutinous rice, green peppers, cinnamon, nutmeg, almonds, hot and spicy foods, leeks and onions, liquor, mushrooms, peanuts, persimmons, pig's knuckles and pork liver, red foods (beans, peppers, tomatoes, etc.) sesame oil, shellfish, sour foods, tangerines, vinegar and wine

(Source : Wan, Liv, "The Yin and Yang in Chinese Cooking," Updated 04/04/17,Retrieved 15 Jan 2018 from https://www.thespruce.com/yin-and-yang-in-chinese-cooking-4062261)

5) Mise en Place

Mise en place (MEEZ ahn plahs) is a French term for having all your ingredients measured, cut, peeled, sliced, grated, etc. before you start cooking. Pans are prepared. Mixing bowls, tools and equipment set out. It is a technique chefs use to assemble meals so quickly and effortlessly (Henneman, 2017)

Practicing mise en place has several benefits:

① Any missing ingredients can be spotted before it's too late for a quick trip to the store or your neighbor next door.

② Special preparation for ingredients—such as toasting nuts, letting certain ingredients come to room temperature, etc.—can be handled BEFORE cooking rather than in the midst of another preparation step when time delays may affect food quality.

③ There is time to clean the mixing area as you go along rather than face a counter full of mixing equipment when you're done.

④ You can group ingredients or place them in the order used to assure all recipe steps are included.

⑤ It makes complicated recipes more fun to prepare when you're no longer doing a juggling act, trying to complete several tasks simultaneously.

Description : Mise en place for hot station in a professional kitchen.

(Source : Retrieved 26 Jan 2018 from https://commons.wikimedia.org/wiki/File:Mise_en_place_for_hot_station.jpg)

6) Aroma vs Smell vs Taste vs Flavor

Aroma is defined as a strong pleasant smell, usually from food or drink. Smell is defined the quality of something that can be detected by the sensitive nerves in the nose. Taste is defined as the sensation or perception of certain qualities of substances put in the mouth, primarily sweet, sour, salt and bitter. Flavor is defined as an identifiable or distinctive quality of food or drink perceived with the combined senses of taste and smell (Dictionary.cambridge, n.d.).

7) Umami

Umami or savory taste, is one of the five basic tastes (together with sweetness, sourness, bitterness, and saltiness). It has been described as brothy or meaty. People taste umami through taste receptors that typically respond to glutamate. Glutamate is widely present in meat broths and fermented products, and commonly added to some foods in the form of monosodium glutamate (MSG). Since umami has its own receptors rather than arising out of a combination of the traditionally recognized taste receptors, scientists now consider umami to be a distinct taste (Wikipedia, 2017).

Description : Picture of tomatoes at the market

(Source : Retrieved 26 Jan 2018 from https://commons.wikimedia.org/wiki/File:Ripe_tomatoes.JPG)

8) Taste buds

We taste with our 'taste buds'. If you look in a mirror you can see these; they are in the tiny bumps that are all over your tongue and the inside of your mouth. Taste buds are clumps of around 100 taste cells. These taste cells respond to types of chemicals and give rise to one of six tastes such as sweet, sour salty, bitter, and spicy and umami (or savory) (Eu-sol, n.d.).

9) Palate vs Texture

Palate is defined as a person's ability to taste and judge good food and wine (Dictionary.cambridge, n.d.), and texture is the feeling of the food in your mouth. In practice texture is not just one thing but lots of different sensations felt all at once.

Food scientists have tried to categorize different aspects of texture to understand what any item of food gives its particular feeling in our mouth.

Here are some below (Eu-sol, n.d.):

① Juiciness—how much liquid is released when the food is crushed between molars?

② Firmness—how easy it is to squeeze?

③ Mealiness—how 'powdery' is the food e.g. cooked potato can be very mealy.

④ Toughness—how resistant the food is to puncture? This is similar to how easy is it to bite into.

⑤ Chewiness—how many chews does it take to reduce the food to a condition where it can be swallowed?

⑥ Elasticity—how much can the food be squeezed and still return to its original shape?

⑦ Meltiness—how quickly does the food dissolve in your mouth?

10) Maillard reaction

The Maillard reaction is many small, simultaneous chemical reactions that occur when proteins and sugars in and on your food are transformed by heat, producing new flavors, aromas, and colors (Schulze, 2017). It is named after French chemist Louis-Camille Maillard, who first described it in 1912 while attempting to reproduce biological protein synthesis (Wikipedia, 2017).

Many popular foods owe their roasted umami flavor to the Maillard Reaction. Many popular foods undergo this culinary phenomenon during cooking.

Here's a small list of products with Maillard reactions (Alfaro, 2017; Scienceofcooking, n.d.).

① Caramel made from milk and sugar

② The dark brown crusts of bagels, pretzels, and toast

③ The color of beer, chocolate, coffee, and maple syrup

④ Self-tanning products

⑤ The flavor of roast meat; Browning of meats

⑥ The color of dried or condensed milk

⑦ The color of garlic; Black garlic

⑧ Golden brown color of french fries

For it to occur, water cannot be present, because water lowers the highest temperature that is possible. A Maillard Reaction starts at about 50℃ (122°F), but goes through 3 stages, with the final browning stage only kicking in at 154℃ (309°F.) Meat in boiling water won't get hotter than the boiling point of water, 100℃ / 212°F, which is why boiled meat doesn't brown. Oil will get hotter though than 154℃ (309°F), which is why meat fried in oil is able to brown.

Even though roasted meat still has water actually inside it, the surface of the meat loses its water through evaporation, enabling a Maillard Reaction to occur on the surface.

A Maillard Reaction is not the same as Caramelization; Caramelization is just sugar on its own breaking down. A Maillard Reaction gives a more complex flavor than Caramelization, because more compounds are required for it to occur (Oulton, 2007).

Description : The crusts of most breads, such as this brioche, are golden-brown due to the Maillard reaction.

(Source : Retrieved 26 Jan 2018 from https://en.wikipedia.org/wiki/Maillard_reaction#/media/File:Brioche.jpg)

11) Foodie vs Gourmet vs Gourmand

Although the two terms "foodie and gourmet" are sometimes used interchangeably, foodies differ from gourmets in that gourmets are epicures of refined taste who may or may not be professionals in the culinary industry, whereas foodies are amateurs who simply love food for consumption, study, preparation, and news.

Gourmets simply want to eat the best food, whereas foodies want to learn everything about food, both the best and the ordinary, and about the science, industry, and personalities surrounding food. For this reason, foodies are sometimes viewed as obsessively interested in all things culinary. There is also a general feeling in the culinary industry that the term gourmet is outdated (Gocalaverasfoodie, n.d.).

Then a gourmand is a person who takes great pleasure and interest in consuming good food and drink. A gourmand has also been defined as a person who is "a glutton for food and drink," a person who eats and drinks excessively (Wikipedia, 2018).

12) Decorate vs Garnish

The word decorate is defined as adding something to an object or place, especially in order to make it more attractive. The word garnish is defined as decorating food with a small amount of different food (Dictionary.cambridge, n.d.).

13) Vegetarian vs Vegan

The Vegetarian Society defines a vegetarian as follows: "A vegetarian is someone who lives on a diet of grains, pulses, legumes, nuts, seeds, vegetables, fruits, fungi, algae, yeast and/or some other non-animal-based foods (e.g. salt) with, or without, dairy products, honey and/or eggs. A vegetarian does not eat foods that consist of, or have been produced with the aid of products consisting of or created from, any part of the body of a living or dead animal. This includes meat, poultry, fish, shellfish, insects, by-products of slaughter or any food made with processing aids created from these."(Vegsoc, n.d.)

There are different types of vegetarian:

① Lacto-ovo-vegetarians eat both dairy products and eggs; this is the most common type of vegetarian diet.

② Lacto-vegetarians eat dairy products but avoid eggs.

③ Ovo-vegetarian eats eggs but not dairy products.

④ Vegans do not eat dairy products, eggs, or any other products which are derived from animals. Some vegans also avoid other animal products such as beeswax, leather or silk clothing, and goose-fat shoe polish (Wikipedia, 2017).

14) American Culinary Federation

The American Culinary Federation (ACF) was established in 1929 and is the largest professional chefs' organization in North America. ACF, which was the progeny of the combined visions of three chefs' associations in New York City, comprises more than 22,000 members in 230 chapters across the United States, and is known as the authority on cooking in America. Its mission is to make a positive difference for culinarians through education, apprenticeship and certification, while creating a fraternal bond of respect and integrity among culinarians everywhere. One of ACF's defining historical moments remains the ACF-led initiative that resulted in the upgrade of the definition of chef from domestic to professional in 1976. The ACF is a member of the World Association of Chefs Societies (Wikipedia, 2017).

15) National Restaurant Association

The National Restaurant Association is a restaurant industry business association in the United States, representing more than 380,000 restaurant locations. It also operates the National Restaurant Association Educational Foundation. The association was founded in 1919 and is headquartered in Washington, DC (Wikipedia, 2017).

16) Restaurant magazine

Restaurant Magazine is a British magazine aimed at chefs, restaurant proprietors and other catering professionals that concentrates on the fine dining end of the Restaurant industry. It was founded in 2001. The magazine is published monthly by William Reed Business Media and had a circulation of 16,642 in December 2011.

It produces an annual list of what it considers to be the best 50 restaurants in the world, based on the votes of 837 "chefs, restaurateurs, critics and fun-loving gourmands" (Wikipedia, 2017).

Note

- meticulous : very thorough and with careful attention to detail
- classique : classic, a classic work of art, literature etc.
- Henri Gault : Henri Gault (4 November 1929 - 9 July 2000) was a French food journalist. He was co-founder of the Gault Millau guides with Christian Millau, and invented the phrase "nouvelle cuisine", though later he claimed to regret it.
- André Gayot : André Gayot is a French journalist.
- Christian Millau : Christian Dubois-Millot, pen name Christian Millau (30 December 1928 – 5 August 2017), was a French food critic and author.
- Gault-Millau : Gault et Millau [go e mijo] is a French restaurant guide. It was founded by two restaurant critics, Henri Gault and Christian Millau in 1965.
- epidemiological : 유행[전염]병학(상)의
- coronary heart disease (CHD) : 관상 동맥성 심장 질환
- saturated fats : 포화 지방
- macrobiotic : Constituting, relating to, or following a diet of whole pure prepared foods that is based on Taoist principles of the balance of yin and yang.
- Zen Buddhism : 선종(禪宗) (달마의 선(禪)에 의해 불도를 터득하는 종파)
- juggling act : An attempt to deal with several conflicting situations, requirements, or pressures at the same time
- epicure : someone who enjoys good food and drink
- glutton : someone who eats much more than they need
- slaughter : the killing of animals, usually for their meat
- progeny : a person's child or children

2. New Phenomena and Concepts

1) Slow food

Slow Food is a grassroots organization founded by Carlo Petrini in Italy in 1986. It has since spread worldwide. Promoted as an alternative to fast food, it strives to preserve traditional and regional cuisine and encourages farming of plants, seeds, and livestock characteristic of the local ecosystem. It was the first established part of the broader slow movement. Its goals of sustainable foods and promotion of local small businesses are paralleled by a political agenda directed against globalization of agricultural products (Wikipedia, 2017).

2) Molecular gastronomy

The term "molecular gastronomy" was coined in 1988 by late Oxford physicist Nicholas Kurti and the French INRA chemist Hervé This. Some chefs associated with the term choose to reject its use, preferring other terms such as multi-sensory cooking, modernist cuisine, culinary physics, and experimental cuisine.

Molecular gastronomy is a subdiscipline of food science that seeks to investigate the physical and chemical transformations of ingredients that occur in cooking. Its program includes three axes, as cooking was recognized to have three components, which are social, artistic and technical. Molecular cuisine is a modern style of cooking, and takes advantage of many technical innovations from the scientific disciplines (Wikipedia, 2017).

Though molecular gastronomy is based on science it is still a mix of science and art of cooking. The scientific component is best understood if we look at techniques, tools and ingredients used for cooking which are summarized below (See Table 7-2; Jez, 2015).

Table 7-2 Molecular gastronomy techniques, tools and ingredients

Techniques	
• Spherification – for producing a caviar-like spheres with new flavors (apple, olive oil …)	
• Aromatic component – gases trapped in a bag, a serving device, or the food itself	
• Whimsical or avant-garde presentation style	
• Unusual flavor combinations, such as combining savory and sweet and flavor juxtaposition	
• Flash freezing	• The use of emulsifiers
• Creating new food textures (gels, foams, glass like food)	
• Cooking in a microwave for creating dishes that are cold or even frozen on the outside with a hot liquid in the center	
• High pressure cooking	• Improved temperature control
• High-power mixing and cutting machines for example ultrasonic agitation to create emulsions	
Tools	
• Liquid nitrogen, for flash freezing without allowing the formation of large ice crystals. Also used for freezing and shattering	
• Anti-griddle (chilled metal top), for cooling and freezing	
• Well controlled water baths for low temperature cooking	
• Food dehydrator	• Centrifuge
• Syringe, for injecting unexpected fillings	• Ultrasound
• Vacuum machine	• Pressure cookers
• pH meters	• Tabletop distilleries
Ingredients	
• Gelling agents like methylcellulose	• Sugar substitutes
• Emulsifiers like soy lecithin and xanthan gum	
• Non-stick agents	
• Enzymes, for example transglutaminase — a protein binder, also called meat glue	
• Carbon dioxide, for adding bubbles and making foams	
• Hydrocolloids such as starch, gelatin, pectin and natural gums — used as thickening agents, gelling agents, emulsifying agents and stabilizers, sometimes needed for foams	

(Source : Jez, Mojca, "Molecular Gastronomy – The Food Science," September 24, 2015, Retrieved 14 Jan 2018 from https://splice-bio.com/molecular-gastronomy-the-food-science/)

3) Food miles

An interesting concept related to carbon footprints is that of "food miles"—the distance food travels from where it is grown to where it is ultimately purchased or consumed by the end user. The more food miles that attach to a given food, the less sustainable and the less environmentally desirable that food is. The term food miles has become part of the vernacular among food system professionals when describing the farm to consumer pathways of food.

Food miles is a term which refers to the distance food is transported from the time of its production until it reaches the consumer. Food miles are one factor used when assessing the environmental impact of food, including the impact on global warming (Wikipedia, 2017).

For example, for every calorie of carrot, flown in from South Africa, we use 66 calories of fuel. The huge fuel use in the food system means more carbon dioxide emissions, which means climate change, which means more damage to food supplies, as well as other major health and social problems (Church, 2005).

At first glance reducing food miles seems an excellent way to reduce carbon emissions, because it limits emissions caused by planes, trucks, boats and trains moving food.But if you're not careful cutting food miles can easily increase your food's carbon footprint.

The most important thing to remember about food miles is that they are only part of the bigger food emissions story. A person's foodprint is actually dominated by production emissions, and food transport makes up just a tenth of food emissions up to the point of sale.

A few different studies have verified this, perhaps the best of which is the 2008 paper by Weber and Matthews, Food-Miles and the Relative Climate Impacts of Food Choices in the United States.Their analysis of US food emissions found 83% of carbon emissions in the food system result from food production, 5% from wholesaling and retailing food, and 11% from transporting it.

Perhaps most interestingly, just 4% of total emissions were final delivery transport from the producer to the retailer, which is what most people think of when they talk about food miles. The point is food miles are only a small part of a very large food emissions story, so focusing on them in isolation isn't necessarily helpful if your goal is to cut your foodprint (See Figure 7-1).

In fact what you eat is generally more important than where it comes from, as is how much you waste (Wilson, n.d.).

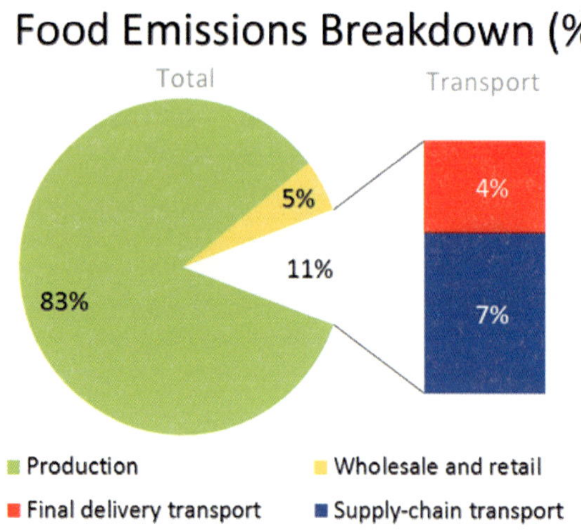

[Figure 7-1] Food Emission Breakdown
(Source : Wilson, Lindsay, "The tricky truth about food miles," Retrieved 14 Jan 2018 from http://shrinkthatfootprint.com/food-miles)

4) Sustainable cuisine

Sustainable cuisine is much more than just 'food miles'. Sustainable cuisine is an environmentally sustainable food system that uses food products grown, harvested, processed, packaged and shipped or distributed with the minimal environmental impact. These boundaries typically mean products meeting the criteria are local or organic (AZoCleantech, 2008).

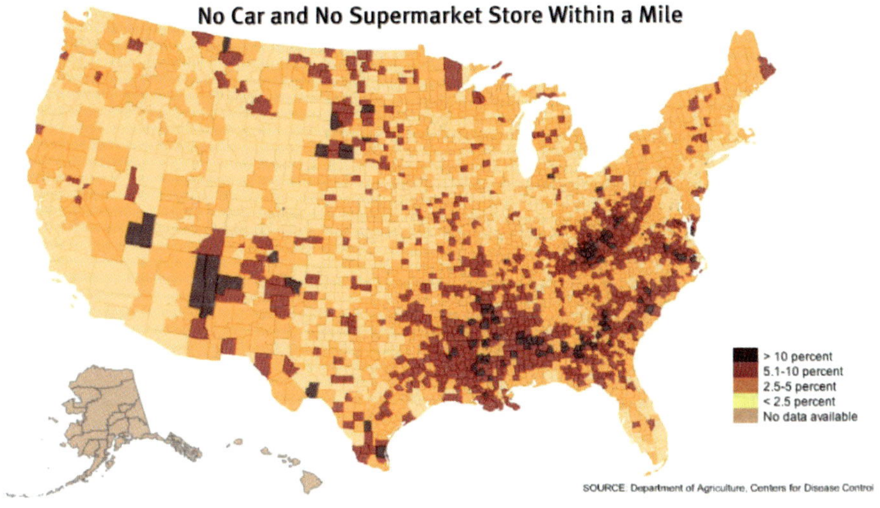

Description : 2016 USDA map. According to the Medley Food Desert Project[citation needed], nearly 24 million Americans live in food deserts. Food deserts are heavily concentrated in southern states, which correlates with concentration of poverty. The map presents percentages of people without cars living in areas with no supermarket within a mile.

(Source : Retrieved 26 Jan 2018 from https://en.wikipedia.org/wiki/Food_desert#/media/File:Data_on_food_deserts.png)

5) Food deserts

Food deserts can be described as geographic areas where residents' access to affordable, healthy food options (especially fresh fruits and vegetables) is restricted or nonexistent due to the absence of grocery stores within convenient travelling distance. For instance, according to a report prepared for Congress by the Economic Research Service of the US Department of Agriculture, about 2.3 million people (or 2.2 percent of all US households) live more than one mile away from a supermarket and do not own a car (Foodispower, n.d.).

6) Culinary tourism

Culinary or food tourism is the pursuit of unique and memorable eating and drinking experiences, both near and far (World Food Travel Association, 2017). It is the exploration of food as the purpose of tourism. It is now considered a vital component of the tourism experience. Dining out is common among tourists and "food is believed to rank alongside climate, accommodation, and scenery" in importance to tourists (McKercher, 2008).

7) Pop-Up Restaurants

According to the association's What's Hot survey, 56% of respondents say pop-up restaurants are still a viable trend (NRA, 2017). Pop-up restaurants, also called supper clubs, are temporary restaurants (Wikipedia, 2018).

Back in the 1960s, the term "supper club" referred to traditional restaurants that also served as exclusive social clubs. They would present themselves as "high-class," even if the price was relatively affordable. Eventually, the term "underground restaurants" became synonymous with "supper clubs." These were "closed door restaurants" where famous chefs would cook food out of their home for the masses—or at least, for those who were "in the know" about the event. In 2007, Ludo Lefebvre brought the underground restaurant concept to the public with one of the first pop-up restaurant concepts: LudoBites, in Los Angeles. LudoBites was a series of temporary eateries that appeared all across LA, seemingly by random—a few days here, a few weeks there—and then disappeared (Tetreault, 2016).

There are several different reasons for opening a pop up restaurant. Some professional chefs open their own pop ups to build their culinary reputation, since the short-term nature of a pop up allows chefs total freedom and creativity in the kitchen. Others open a pop up restaurant to test out a restaurant concept, using it as an avenue to entice investors as well as the public to try it out. On a more philosophical note, other people use pop up restaurants as a way to offer gourmet dining at reduced prices, so everyone can enjoy it. Lastly, pop ups are sometimes used as a vehicle for fundraising by civic and community groups (Mealey, 2017).

Note

- vernacular : the language spoken by a particular group or in a particular area, when it is different from the formal written language
- spherification : the process of forming something into a sphere or spheres
- whimsical : playfully quaint or fanciful, especially in an appealing and amusing way
- avant-garde : new and unusual or experimental ideas, especially in the arts, or the people introducing them
- juxtaposition : the fact of two things being seen or placed close together with contrasting effect
- emulsifier : 유화제(乳化劑)
- agitation : the action of briskly stirring or disturbing something, especially a liquid
- centrifuge : 원심 분리기
- tabletop distillery : 탁상용 증류기
- hydrocolloid : 하이드로콜로이드, 친수(親水) 콜로이드, 수성콜로이드
- thickening agents : 농후제
- gelling agents : 겔화제
- emulsifying agents : 유화제
- stabilizers : 안정제
- Ludo Lefebvre : Ludovic "Ludo" Lefebvre, born 18 April 1971, is a French chef, restaurateur, pop-up impresario, author, and television personality.

References

Alfaro, Danilo, "What is the Maillard Reaction?" 09/18/17, Retrieved 15 Jan 2018from https://www.thespruce.com/what-is-the-maillard-reaction-995776

AZoCleantech, "Sustainable Cuisine, What Is Sustainable Cuisine and What BenefitsDoes it Offer for Improving the Quality of Food, Health and the Environment," 2008, Retrieved 13 Jan 2018 from https://www.azocleantech.com/article.aspx?ArticleID=114

Church, Norman, "Why Our Food is So Dependent on Oil, 01 April 2005, Retrieved14 Jan 2018 from https://100777.com/node/1236

Eu-sol, "What is taste?/What is texture?," Retrieved Jan. 4, 2010 from http://www.eu-sol.net/

Foodispower, "Food deserts," Retrieved 12 Jan 2018 from http://www.foodispower.org/food-deserts/

Gocalaverasfoodie, "What is a Foodie?," Retrieved Jan. 4, 2010 from http://gocalaverasfoodie.com/what-is-a-foodie/

Henneman, Alice, "Use "Mise en Place" to Make Meal Preparation Easier," Retrieved 10 Jan 2018 from https://food.unl.edu/use-mise-en-place-make-meal-preparation-easier

Jez, Mojca, "Molecular Gastronomy—The Food Science," September 24, 2015, Retrieved 14 Jan 2018 from https://splice-bio.com/molecular-gastronomy-the-food-science/

McKercher, Bob; Okumus, Fevzi; Okumus, Bendegul (2008). "Food Tourism as a Viable Market Segment: It's All How You Cook the Numbers!". Journal of Travel& Tourism Marketing. 25 (2): 137-148.

Mealey, Lorri, "How to Open a Pop-Up Restaurant," June 23, 2017, Retrieved 26Jan 2018 from https://www.thebalance.com/how-to-open-a-pop-up-restaurant-2888697

Oulton, Randal. "Maillard Reaction." CooksInfo.com. Published 29 Nov 2005; revised30 May 2007, Retrieved 15 Jan 2018 from http://www.cooksinfo.com/maillard-reaction

Schulze, Eric, "An Introduction to the Maillard Reaction: The Science of Browning, Aroma, and Flavor," 2017, Retrieved 15 Jan 2018 from http://www.seriouseats.com/2017/04/what-is-maillard-reaction-cooking-science.html

Scienceofcooking, Why Food Browns, Retrieved 15 Jan 2018 from http://www.scienceofcooking.com/maillard_reaction.htm

Tetreault, Allie, "What is a Pop-Up Restaurant? 20+ Tips, Strategies, and Examples," 12/14/16, Retrieved 26 Jan 2018 from https://pos.toasttab.com/blog/pop-up-restaurants

Vegsoc, "What is a vegetarian?" Retrieved 14 Jan 2018 from https://www.vegsoc.org/definition

Wan, Liv, "The Yin and Yang in Chinese Cooking," Updated 04/04/17, Retrieved 15Jan 2018 from https://www.thespruce.com/yin-and-yang-in-chinese-cooking-4062261

Wilson, Lindsay, "The tricky truth about food miles," Retrieved 14 Jan 2018 from http://shrinkthatfootprint.com/food-miles

World Food Travel Association, "What is Food Tourism?" Retrieved 14 Jan 2018 from https://www.worldfoodtravel.org/cpages/what-is-food-tourism

Retrieved 12 Jan 2018 from https://en.wikipedia.org/wiki/Culinary_tourism

Retrieved 12 Jan 2018 from https://en.wikipedia.org/wiki/Food_miles

Retrieved 12 Jan 2018 from https://en.wikipedia.org/wiki/Restaurant_(magazine)

Retrieved 14 Jan 2018 from https://en.wikipedia.org/wiki/Molecular_gastronomy

Retrieved 14 Jan 2018 from https://en.wikipedia.org/wiki/Slow_Food

Retrieved 14 Jan 2018 from https://en.wikipedia.org/wiki/National_Restaurant_Association

Retrieved 14 Jan 2018 from https://en.wikipedia.org/wiki/Vegetarianism

Retrieved 14 Jan 2018 from https://en.wikipedia.org/wiki/American_Culinary_Federation

Retrieved 15 Jan 2018 from https://en.wikipedia.org/wiki/Maillard_reaction

Retrieved 15 Jan 2018 from https://en.wikipedia.org/wiki/Haute_cuisine

Retrieved 15 Jan 2018 from https://en.wikipedia.org/wiki/Nouvelle_cuisine

Retrieved 15 Jan 2018 from https://en.wikipedia.org/wiki/French_paradox

Retrieved 16 Jan 2018 from https://en.wikipedia.org/wiki/Macrobiotic_diet

Retrieved 16 Jan 2018 from https://en.wikipedia.org/wiki/Umami

Retrieved 16 Jan 2018 from https://en.wikipedia.org/wiki/Gourmand

Retrieved 26 Jan 2018 from https://en.wikipedia.org/wiki/Ludo_Lefebvre

Retrieved 26 Jan 2018 from https://en.wikipedia.org/wiki/Pop-up_restaurant

Retrieved 26 Jan 2018 from http://www.restaurant.org/Downloads/PDFs/News-Research/WhatsHot/What-s-Hot-2017-FINAL

Retrieved Jan 17, 2018 from http://www.answers.com/topic/craft

Retrieved Jan 17, 2018 from http://en.wiktionary.org/,

Retrieved Jan 17, 2018 from https://www.collinsdictionary.com/dictionary/english

Retrieved Jan 17, 2018 from https://dictionary.cambridge.org/

Retrieved Jan 17, 2018 from https://www.oxforddictionaries.com/

Chapter 08

Commitment to Lifelong Learning

Description : President Barack Obama delivers the commencement speech at Hampton University in Hampton, Virginia, May 9, 2010.
(Source: Retrieved 26 Jan 2018 from https://obamawhitehouse.archives.gov/blog/2010/05/10/education-means-emancipation)

"If you don't follow your dream, who will?"

- Emeril Lagasse (born October 15, 1959), an American celebrity chef, restaurateur, television personality, cookbook author, and National Best Recipe award winner for his 'Turkey and Hot Sausage Chili' recipe in 2003

1. A Positive Attitude towards Learning

No matter what level of education you have, if you want to succeed, you need to keep on learning. The information available worldwide doubles every few years, and technology—especially information technology—is part of virtually every workplace. As a result, employers value knowledgeable employees who are committed to lifelong learning (Alberta, 2017)

A successful learner starts with having a positive attitude towards learning. A positive attitude lets you relax, remember, focus and absorb information as you learn. You're ready to welcome new experiences and recognize many different kinds of learning opportunities. And when you can see opportunities, hope increases.

Do you stay open to learning opportunities? Do you believe that you're able to learn new things? Use this exercise to explore your attitudes and beliefs about learning. Put a check mark beside the statements that are true for you:

- I believe lifelong learning will help me achieve my goals.
- I'm willing to make mistakes and learn from them.
- I'm aware that learning opportunities are all around me.
- I take charge of my own learning. I use every opportunity I have to learn something new.
- I'm willing and eager to learn.
- I know what skills and knowledge I need or want to learn.
- I know where to find out about formal learning opportunities through mentors, co-workers, friends, supervisors, family members and my own research.

• I set new learning goals regularly.

How many did you score out of 8 possible check marks? Take a close look at the statements you didn't check off. Think about how these attitudes could be affecting your success as a learner.

For each statement that you didn't check off, think of 2 steps that you could take right now to build a positive learning attitude in this area. For example, if you don't know what skills and knowledge you need to learn, how can you find out? If you're working, could you ask your supervisor? If you're not working, could you talk to a career advisor or find the information online or in a book or magazine?

Formal classroom learning can be important and valuable, but it's only one of many learning opportunities that are open to you. You can learn:

① at work

② on your own

③ from mentors and role models

④ from co-workers and friends

⑤ online by using search engines, following blogs, downloading podcasts, taking a class, etc.

⑥ through magazines, journals, newspapers, videos, broadcasts

⑦ by volunteering

⑧ by teaching others what you know, which helps you improve your skills and insight

⑨ through seminars, workshops and courses

⑩ by attending classes at an educational institution, in person or online

More than ever, learning is for life. All kinds of learning opportunities are just a "click" or a conversation away. A positive attitude and a belief in your ability to keep learning will help you enjoy the process and discover many opportunities along the way.

2. Culinary Education

1) Culinary certification (or certificate) in culinary arts

With thousands of chefs competing in the job market, it is essential to prove your culinary competency. Many community colleges, junior colleges, technical schools,other institutions of higher education, and other culinary associations offer various certification programs in culinary arts. A certification demonstrates skill, knowledge and professionalism to the culinary industry.

With successful completion of the culinary certification program, students earn a certification in culinary arts or a certificate of completion(=achievement). A certificate of achievement requires a commitment of one year if you attend full-time. Many courses are offered so that students can work and attend them part-time (Acfchefs, n.d.; Tmcc, n.d.). But graduation from a well-respected culinary school and experience in well regarded restaurants generally carries more weight than certification (Newfuturesdc, 2009).

Description : Biblioburro, traveling library in Colombia

(Source : Retrieved 28 Jan 2018 from https://commons.wikimedia.org/wiki/File:Biblioburro.jpg)

2) Associate degree (or Associate's degree) in culinary arts

It is, in short, expressed as two-year college degree. It is defined as a degree earned on completion of a two-year program of study at a community college, junior college, technical school, or other institution of higher education. An associate degree requires a two-year commitment if you attend full-time (Tmcc, n.d.).

3) Bachelor's degree in culinary arts

It is defined as a degree awarded on the successful completion of an undergraduate course at a four-year college or university. This gives students additional experience, education and a competitive edge upon entering into the culinary industry (Bic, n.d.).

In general there are two ways to earn a bachelor's degree in culinary arts. The first way is, after high school, to progress to a bachelor's degree program at a four-year college or university. During the first two years of the program, students follow the curriculum for the Associate degree, and the following two years focus on more advanced techniques, as well as the training in management and leadership.

The second one is to transfer to bachelor's degree programs; upon completion of your associate degrees in culinary arts, and then students transfer to a four-year college or university to complete your junior and senior years of a bachelor's degree in culinary arts.

Note

- commitment : something that takes up time or energy, especially an obligation
- podcast : a multimedia file, such as a radio program or music video, that can be downloaded from the Internet and played on an mp3 player or similar piece of equipment. The method of publishing files that can be used in this way is called podcasting
- competency : an important skill that is needed to do a job
- keep up with : to remain abreast of something that undergoes continuous change or progress
- come true : to happen as hoped for
- institution : a large and important organization, such as a university or bank

3. Taking an Overseas Internship

1) Introduction to Culinary Internships

If you're trying to broaden your experiential backgrounds and supplement your academic studies via a hands-on work experience in a hotel or restaurantenvironment, culinary internships are for you. Depending upon colleges or universities culinary students are often required to complete an internship, "externship", or practicum as part of their programs. Academic credit can be earned for a successful internship. Internships are offered in 3-month, 6-month and 12-month durations. Interns may extend the duration of your internship program beyond six months. The minimum duration is three months and a maximum of eighteen months. Approval from the student's college or university may be required. Most internships are unpaid positions but some pay an hourly rate (Jobs.foursesons, n.d.; Learn4good, n.d.).

2) Internship vs Externship

The term internship is a chance to try out a prospective career and to gain professional work experience related to a student's major or career goal. The internship plan generally involves a student working in a professional setting under the supervision and monitoring of practicing professionals. Internships are administered by the individual organization desiring interns, therefore, their structure and policies will vary. Internships can be paid or unpaid, and the student may or may not receive academic credit for performing the internship (Mills, n.d.; Emerson, n.d.; Virginia, n.d.; Ipfw, n.d.).

The word externship designs as a one day job shadowing/mentorship experience, but can be extended longer if you choose. It is an opportunity for students to gain understanding of a business, industry, and/or job function, to ask questions, and to observe first hand day to day business operations. Then what is the difference between an Externship and an Internship? An externship is brief, and offer no pay or academic credit. An internship is usually 3-12 months in duration, and can be paid or for credit (Bc, n.d.).

3) Intern Jobs

Interns are typically assigned to entry-level job classifications based on their background and experience, and their stated personal interests. Culinary internships are temporary positions within hotels or restaurants that allow you to gain practical experience by working alongside professionals. Culinary interns will usually be required to concentrate on one area during your internship in which they have a particular interest or expertise. However, some opportunities for cross-training may be available depending on the size of the hotels and restaurants. Culinary interns will rotate through several kitchen stations including the hot line, hot prep, buffets, banquet kitchens, bake shop, and garde manger. Rotation within departments will be based on the student's abilities and desire to excel. The aim of your internship is to learn the policies, systems and procedures in place for each department you work in (Learn4good, n.d.; Cphiltonhead, n.d.),

4) Benefits

Students interning in hotels or restaurants are encouraged to gain the knowledge, skills and experience that relate directly to your educational program and future career goals. You get the opportunity to apply the knowledge, skills and experience you have gained in real-life situations. This hands-on experience will allow you to make more informed decisions about the career path you take following your graduation (Learn4good, n.d.; Cphiltonhead, n.d.),.

Many hotels or restaurants that offer culinary internship programs will often give preference to former interns. Former interns are also more likely to be offered a full-time position on graduation as you have had the chance to prove your abilities.Culinary interns in hotels may receive other benefits such as on-site accommodation, free meals or the use of swimming pools or other leisure facilities. But in the U.S., housing, salaries and benefits vary from location to location and will be discussed during the interview process. Culinary internships in hotels or restaurants may be more easily obtained in the busier holiday periods ((Learn4good, n.d.; Jobs.foursesons, n.d.).

On the other hand, throughout the course of your internship, you will find ample opportunities to experience the authentic life of other countries. You will discover the vibrant culture of other countries and meet many people and make friends from all over the world.

Note

- supplement : to add something to something to make it larger or better
- hands-on : relating to, being, or providing direct practical experience in the operation or functioning of something <hands-on training>
- practicum : a period of work for practical experience as part of an academic course
- supervision : when someone watches a person or activity and makes certain that everything is done correctly, safely, etc.
- credit : a unit which represents a successfully finished part of an educational course
- shadowing : the act of following someone secretly
- mentorship : a wise and trusted guide and advisor
- entry-level : at the lowest level and suitable for somebody who is new to a job, field, or subject
- garde manger : ① a cool room used for storing foods and for preparing certain dishes, esp. cold buffet dishes. ② a cook who specializes in the preparation of cold foods (as meats, fish, and salads)
- in place : ready for use
- preference : an advantage which is given to a person or a group of people
- accommodation : a place to live, work, stay, etc. in
- ample : more than enough
- vibrant : energetic, exciting and full of enthusiasm

4. Eminent Educational Institutes

1) The Culinary Institute of America

The Culinary Institute of America (CIA) is an American private college and culinary school specializing in culinary, baking, and pastry arts education. The school's primary campus is located in Hyde Park, New York, with branch campuses in St. Helena and Napa, California, San Antonio, Texas, and the Republic of Singapore. The college, which was the first to teach culinary arts in the United States, offers associate and bachelor's degrees, and has the largest staff of American Culinary Federation Certified Master Chefs. The CIA also offers continuing education for professionals in the hospitality industry as well as conferences and consulting services. In addition to professional education, the college also offers recreational classes for non-professionals. The college operates student-run restaurants on their four U.S. campuses.

The school was founded in 1946 in New Haven, Connecticut, as a vocational institute for returning veterans of World War II. With a growing student body, the school purchased a former Jesuit novitiate in Hyde Park in 1970, which remains its central campus. The school began awarding associate degrees in 1971 and bachelor's degrees in 1993. Additional campuses were opened in the following years: St. Helena in 1995, Texas in 2008, Singapore in 2010, and its Napa campus in 2016 (Wikipedia, 2018).

Description : The Gatehouse Restaurant, Greystone's student-run restaurant

(Source : Retrieved 26 Jan 2018 from https://en.wikipedia.org/wiki/The_Culinary_Institute_of_America#/media/File:CIA_at_Greystone_2015_01.png

2) Johnson & Wales University

Johnson & Wales University (JWU) is an American private, nonprofit, co-educational, career-oriented university with one main and three branch campuses located throughout the United States. Providence, Rhode Island is home to JWU's first, largest, and main campus. Founded as a business school in 1914 by Gertrude I. Johnson and Mary T. Wales, JWU currently has 15,063 students enrolled in business, arts & sciences, culinary arts, education, engineering, equine management, hospitality, and engineering technology programs across its campuses.

The university is accredited by the New England Association of Schools & Colleges (NEASC), through its Commission on Institutions of Higher Education (Wikipedia, 2018).

Description : The Cuisinart Center for Culinary Excellence, Harborside campus in Providence
(Source : Retrieved 26 Jan 2018 from https://en.wikipedia.org/wiki/Johnson_%26_Wales_University#/media/File:Johnson_and_Wales_Culinary_building,_Harborside_campus,_Providence_RI.jpg

3) Le Cordon Bleu

Founded in Paris in1895, Le Cordon Bleu earned its reputation as the ultimate in cuisine, patisserie, hospitality and gastronomy training, after a century of dedication to the culinary arts.

Educating over 20,000 students each year, from 70 nationalities, distributed across 50 schools in 20 different countries, Le Cordon Bleu is also home to the finest educators in the fields of cuisine and hospitality — chefs and industry professionals who have reached the pinnacle of their profession (Ko-kr.facebook, 2018).

Description : Le Cordon Bleu Paris culinary school, Paris, France

(Source : Retrieved 26 Jan 2018 from
https://en.wikipedia.org/wiki/Le_Cordon_Bleu#/media/File:Paris_06_2012_Cordon_Bleu_3149.jpg)

4) The Institut Paul Bocuse

A showcase for French know-how and etiquette, Institut Paul Bocuse is presided by two exceptional men: Paul Bocuse, founder of the school in 1990, and Gérard Pélisson, Chairman of the Board of Directors since 1998.

Guided by the inspiration and tireless energy of these two world famous figures, Institut Paul Bocuse welcomes 1000 students from 50 countries distributed on 6 international campus.

Students from 50 different countries have come here for their future; driven by the values and education embodied by Institut Paul Bocuse, the school for jobs in hospitality, foodservice and culinary arts management (Institutpaulbocuse, 2018).

Description : L'Institut de Paul Bocuse - Lyon
(Source : Retrieved 26 Jan 2018 from https://www.novoceram.com/blog/references/linstitut-de-paul-bocuse-lyon

5) Westminster Kingsway College

Westminster Kingsway College is a further education college in central London with centres in King's Cross and Regent's Park in Camden, together with Victoria (1910) and Soho centres in Westminster. The college has around 14,000 students across all age ranges and provides further, adult and higher education programmes including full-time and part-time vocational, professional and academic courses at different levels. 75% of students are over the age of 21 and there are over 60 nationalities and around 50 languages spoken. Students are mainly from London. An international department has students from overseas including those who attend study visits, exchanges and internships from partner colleges overseas (Wikipedia, 2018).

Description : The Soho centre of Westminster Kingsway College.

(Source : Retrieved 26 Jan 2018 from ttps://en.wikipedia.org/wiki/Westminster_Kingsway_hCollege#/media/File:Hopkins_Street,_Soho_02.JPG

6) Blue Elephant Cooking School (Bangkok, Thailand)

After setting up the Blue Elephant restaurants in Brussels (1980), London (1986), Copenhagen (1990) and Paris (1991), Chef Nooror and her husband discovered the Old Thai Chine Building in Bangkok, in the year 2000. They instantly fell in love with its unique architecture, history and location.

Cited by the Fine Arts Department, the building is an exceptional example of the colonial era architecture. Partially renovated in 2000, the building was fully restored in 2002 to launch the Blue Elephant Cooking School and Restaurant. Chef Nooror and her husband Mr. Steppe's dream to develop and train chefs to understand and spread the Blue Elephant culinary philosophy finally took wing.

The Blue Elephant Cooking School invites participants to discover, relish and replicate the many culinary wonders of Royal Thai cuisine. Our classrooms are fully equipped with the necessary facilities. You will be guided by an experienced and knowledgeable instructor.

A typical day at our schools will commence with a visit to the morning market accompanied by our instructor, where you will learn to carefully choose the right ingredients for your own home cooking. This is followed by the instructor-led class. The session ends with a delightful meal in our restaurant. There you will sample your own cooking (Blueelephantcookingschool, 2018).

Description : The Thai Chine Building

(Source : Retrieved 26 Jan 2018 from http://blueelephantcookingschool.com/bangkok/files/2016

Note

- Jesuit novitiate : 예수회소유 건물
- equine : relating to or affecting horses or other members of the horse family
- gastronomy : the practice or art of choosing, cooking, and eating good food.
- pinnacle : the highest point of development or achievement
- preside : to be in charge of an official meeting, ceremony, or other event
- relish : to like or enjoy something
- replicate : to make or do something again in exactly the same way
- commence : to begin, or to begin something

References

Acfchefs, "Certification Designations," Retrieved Jan. 14, 2010 from http://www.acfchefs.org/Content/NavigationMenu2/Careers/Certification/Designations/default.htm

Acfchefs, "certification," Retrieved Jan. 7, 2010 from http://www.acfchefs.org/Content/NavigationMenu2/Careers/Certification/default.htm

Alberta, "A Positive Attitude Will Help You Learn," 2017, Retrieved 15 Jan 2018from https://alis.alberta.ca/succeed-at-work/explore-ways-to-improve-your-work/a-positive-attitude-will-help-you-learn/

Bic, "Bachelor of Science in Culinary Management," Retrieved Jan. 7, 2010 from http://www.bic.edu/programs/school-of-culinary-arts/bachelors-degree

Bc, "Externship program," Retrieved Jan. 7, 2010 from http://www.bc.edu/offices/careers/employers/externship.html

Blueelephantcookingschool,, "About Us," Retrieved 15 Jan 2018 from http://blueelephantcookingschool.com/bangkok/about-us/

Cphiltonhead, "Internship Program," Retrieved Feb. 2, 2010 from http://www.cphiltonhead.com/cp/Career-Opportunities-Internships-Hilton-Head-Island-SC.htm

Emerson, "Internships," Retrieved Jan. 7, 2010 from http://www.emerson.edu/media_arts/VMA-Internships.cfm

Institutpaulbocuse, History," Retrieved 15 Jan 2018 from http://www.institutpaulbocuse.com/en/the-institut-paul-bocuse/history/

Jobs.foursesons, "Your four seasons future," Retrieved Feb. 2, 2010 from http://jobs.fourseasons.com/Jobs/faq/Pages/FAQs.aspx

Learn4good, "Hotel Internship Programs," Retrieved Feb. 3, 2010 from http://www.learn4good.com/internships/hotel_internship_programs.htm

Mills, "Internships: "General Information," Retrieved Jan. 7, 2010 from http://www.mills.edu/academics/internships/index.php

Newfuturesdc, 2009, 2009-2010 Career Guide; Promising Careers that Don't Require Four

Years of College, New Futures, Retrieved Feb. 5, 2010 from http://www.newfuturesdc.org/wp-content/uploads/2009/11/Career-Guide.pdf

Tmcc, "Culinary Arts Degree and Certificates," Retrieved Jan. 7, 2010 from http://www.tmcc.edu/culinary/degrees/

Virginia, "Internships: Frequently Asked Questions," Retrieved Jan. 7, 2010 from http://www.career.virginia.edu/students/programs/internship/faq.php

Retrieved 15 Jan 2018 from https://en.wikipedia.org/wiki/The_Culinary_Institute_of_America

Retrieved 15 Jan 2018 from https://en.wikipedia.org/wiki/Johnson_%26_Wales_University

Retrieved 15 Jan 2018 from https://ko-kr.facebook.com/pg/LeCordonBleuAustralia/about/?ref=page_internal

Retrieved 15 Jan 2018 from https://en.wikipedia.org/wiki/Westminster_Kingsway_College

Retrieved Jan 18, 2018 from http://encarta.msn.com/

Retrieved Jan 18, 2018 from http://www.merriam-webster.com/dictionary/

Retrieved Jan 18, 2018 from http://dictionary.cambridge.org/

Retrieved Jan 18, 2018 from http://www.answers.com/topic/craft

Retrieved Jan 18, 2018 from http://en.wiktionary.org/

Retrieved Jan 18, 2018 from https://www.collinsdictionary.com/dictionary/english

Retrieved Jan 18, 2018 from https://dictionary.cambridge.org/

Retrieved Jan 18, 2018 from https://www.oxforddictionaries.com/

Chapter 09

The Best Restaurants

Description : noma Restaurant in Copenhagen - Main Entrance
(Source : Retrieved 26 Jan 2018 from https://commons.wikimedia.org/wiki/File:Noma_entrance.jpg)

"If it doesn't taste good it doesn't go on the menu."

- Heston Blumenthal (born 27 May 1966), a British celebrity chef

1. Michelin 3-star restaurants by Michelin Guide

Table 9-1 shows a short list of Michelin 3-star restaurants by country as of 2017. This section introduces 5 Michelin 3-star restaurants such as Le Louis XV, Per Se, Masa, Benu, and Sukiyabashi Jiro according to author's selection criteria.

Table 9-1 List of Michelin 3-star restaurants by country (as of 2017)

Name of nation	Number of restaurant	Remarks
Belgium	2	
China	10	Shanghai(2), Hong Kong(6), Macau(2)
Denmark	1	
France	27	
Germany	11	
Italy	9	
Japan	34	
Monaco	1	
Netherlands	3	
Norway	1	
Singapore	1	
South Korea	2	
Spain	11	
Switzerland	3	
United Kingdom	5	
United States	13	

(Source : Retrieved Jan. 19, 2018 from https://en.wikipedia.org/wiki/List_of_Michelin_3-star_restaurants)

1) Le Louis XV (restaurant)

Le Louis XV is a French restaurant in Monte Carlo, Monaco. Run by chef Alain Ducasse, it holds three Michelin stars. It has been featured in lists of the world's top restaurants.

Le Louis XV is the flagship restaurant of chef Alain Ducasse. It is located inside the Hôtel de Paris Monte-Carlo, in Monte Carlo, Monaco. He opened the restaurant in May 1987, having been challenged by Prince Rainier III of Monaco and the Société des bains de mer de Monaco to win three Michelin stars there within four years, becoming the first hotel-based restaurant to win that level of the award. Ducasse won the three stars for the restaurant 33 months later, some fifteen months earlier than his objective.

The wine cellar contains around 400,000 bottles of wine. A number of food trolleys are used by the waiters, including for champagne, cheese and one holding herbs to make herbal teas at the tableside.

Several chefs who went on to lead Michelin starred restaurants underwent training at Le Louis XV, including Alexis Gauthier and Clare Smyth.

Description : Restaurant Louis XV. Hotel de Paris, Monaco. August 2016.

(Source : Retrieved 26 Jan 2018 from https://commons.wikimedia.org/wiki/File:2016_Hotel_de_Paris_-_Monaco_03_Restaurant_Louis_XV.jpg)

2) Per Se (restaurant)

Opened in 2004, Per Se is Thomas Keller's acclaimed New York interpretation of The French Laundry in the Time Warner Center at Columbus Circle. Designed by Adam D. Tihany, Per Se features a serene and intimate environment with spectacular views of Central Park and Columbus Circle.

The restaurant is Chef Keller's second three-Michelin-starred property featuring his daily nine-course tasting menu and a nine-course vegetable tasting menu using classic French technique and the finest quality ingredients available. An award-winning wine list, boasting more than 2,000 bottles, complements the menu. The list highlights a collection of older wines as well as wines from small producers that are released in limited quantities. Per Se is a member of French-based associated Relais & Chateaux, Relais Gourmands and Traditions & Qualité organizations, recognized for their dedication to maintaining the highest international standards for hospitality and culinary excellence.

3) Masa (restaurant)

Masa (雅) is a Japanese and sushi restaurant located on the fourth floor of the Time Warner Center at 10 Columbus Circle (at West 60th Street and Broadway) in Manhattan in New York City.

The restaurant was opened by Chef Masa Takayama in 2004 and is considered one of the most expensive restaurants in the world, as well as the most expensive restaurant in New York City. Located next door to the restaurant is Bar Masa, a more accessible dining experience offering an à la carte menu. In 2009, a second Bar Masa opened inside Aria in Las Vegas.

The offerings are Omakase (no menu) only, with chef-selected meals costing US$595 per person, not including tax or drinks, though gratuity is included. The sushi bar itself is a US$260,000 piece of rare hinoki wood from Japan; Masa is one of only two sushi restaurants in North America to have a hinoki wood sushi bar. Reservations for the 26 available seats are taken three weeks in advance. Chef Masa Takayama prepares the menu himself, often including seasonal ingredients. He uses many exotic ingredients, such as truffles and Kobe beef. Most of the fish is flown in from Japan. Chef Masa can be seen working behind the bar and will sometimes serve the food as well. While there is no menu to order from, Chef Masa does keep a record of what he has served to his customers and what their reactions were so he can cater to them on their next visit.

Masa garnered the Michelin Guide's highest rating starting with the 2009 guide and was the first Japanese restaurant in the U.S. to do so. It received three out of four stars by The New York Times. It has also received five out of five stars in the Forbes Travel Guide (formerly known as the Mobil Guide). It has been named as one of New York's Top 50 by Travel + Leisure. Forbes named Masa as the Most Expensive Restaurant In The U.S. for 2005 through 2009 as well as The World's Most Expensive Sushi in 2007 through 2009.

Description : Front view of Masa

(Source : Retrieved 26 Jan 2018 from http://food.allwomenstalk.com/of-the-worlds-best-michelin-star-restaurants)

4) Benu

Benu is a restaurant located in the SoMa district of downtown San Francisco opened in 2010 by Corey Lee. In 2014, Benu was awarded three stars from the Michelin Guide.

Lee was formerly head chef at The French Laundry and draws from many different cuisines, including Cantonese and Korean.

Benu is housed on the ground floor of a historic building that dates back to 1922-originally the headquarters of the San Francisco Newspaper Company. Crown Point Press, an art studio, gallery, and bookstore, now owns the building and resides directly above the restaurant.

In 2015, Phaidon published Benu—a collection of recipes and essays that explores the restaurant's food, influences, and collaborators—with forwards by Thomas Keller and David Chang, designed by Julia Hasting.

Benu currently holds the highest Michelin Guide rating possible: three stars. Lee earned 4 Stars from the San Francisco Chronicle in 2012 (Bauer, 2012). Benu has been assigned Five Diamond Award by AAA since 2012 (AAA, 2017). In 2017, he was nominated 2017 Best Chef West: West (CA, HI, NV) by James Beard Foundation (JBF Editors, 2017).

Description : View of the Benu kitchen from outside

(Source : Retrieved 27 Jan 2018 from https://commons.wikimedia.org/wiki/File:Benu.Street_View.Eric_Wolfinger.jpg)

5) Sukiyabashi Jiro

Sukiyabashi Jiro (すきやばし次郎? Sukiyabashi Jirō) is a sushi restaurant in Ginza, Chūō, Tokyo, Japan. It is owned and operated by sushi master Jiro Ono. The Michelin Guide has awarded it 3 stars. A two-star branch operated by his son Takashi is located at Roppongi Hills in Minato, Tokyo. French chef Joël Robuchon says that the restaurant is one of his favorites in the world, and that it taught him that sushi is an art. Sukiyabashi Jiro was the subject of David Gelb's 2011 documentary film Jiro Dreams of Sushi.

U.S. President Barack Obama dined at the restaurant with Japanese Prime Minister Shinzō Abe on April 23, 2014. There are conflicting reports as to whether he finished the sushi, though Prime Minister Abe said "Obama proclaimed it 'the best sushi I've ever had in my life (Wikipedia, 2018).'"

Description : President Barack Obama and Prime Minister Shinzo Abe of Japan talk with sushi master Jiro Ono, owner of Sukiyabashi Jiro sushi restaurant, during a dinner in Tokyo, Japan, April 23, 2014. (Official White House Photo by Pete Souza)

(Source : Retrieved 27 Jan 2018 from https://commons.wikimedia.org/wiki/File:Barack_Obama_and_Shinzo_Abe_at_Sukyabashi_Jiro_April_2014.jpg)

Note

- Monte Carlo : a town and popular resort in the principality of Monaco; world-famous for its gambling casino
- Alain Ducasse : Alain Ducasse (French: [alɛ̃ dykas]; born 13 September 1956) is a French-born Monégasque chef. He operates a number of restaurants including Alain Ducasse at The Dorchester which holds three stars (the top ranking) in the Michelin Guide.
- flagship : the best or most important product, idea, building, etc. that an organization owns or produces
- the Hôtel de Paris Monte-Carlo : The Hôtel de Paris Monte-Carlo is a hotel located in Monaco, It was opened in 1863 as part of the development of Monaco by the Société des Bains de Mer (SBM) under the auspices of Charles III of Monaco.
- Prince Rainier III : Rainier III (born Rainier Louis Henri Maxence Bertrand Grimaldi; 31 May 1923 – 6 April 2005) ruled the Principality of Monaco for almost 56 years, making him one of the longest ruling monarchs in European history. Though internationally known for his marriage to American actress Grace Kelly, he was also responsible for reforms to Monaco's constitution and for expanding the principality's economy beyond its traditional casino gambling base. Gambling accounts for only approximately three percent of the nation's annual revenue today; when Rainier ascended the throne in 1949, it accounted for more than 95 percent.
- the Société des bains de mer de Monaco : The Société des Bains de Mer (pronounced [sɔsjete də bɛ̃ də mɛː ʁ]), officially the Société des Bains de Mer et du Cercle des Étrangers à Monaco (pronounced [sɔsjete də bɛ̃ də mɛː ʁ du seʁle de etʁɑ̃geʁ ɑ mɔnako]), abbreviated SBM; Euronext: BAIN is a publicly traded company registered in the Principality of Monaco. SBM manages and owns the Monte Carlo Casino, the Opéra de Monte-Carlo, and the Hotel de Paris in Monte Carlo.
- trolley : a cart or wheeled stand used for conveying something (such as food or books)
- Alexis Gauthier : Alexis Pascal Gauthier (born 24 June 1973) is a French chef. He

is the chef patron of the Gauthier Soho restaurant in Soho, London and was awarded a Michelin star in 2011. He previously held a Michelin star as head chef of the restaurant Roussillon in Pimlico, London, until 2010. He was trained under Alain Ducasse at Le Louis XV in Monaco, and has appeared as a judge on two versions of the BBC One television show MasterChef.

- Clare Smyth : Clare Smyth MBE (born 1978) is a Northern Irish chef. She was Chef Patron at Restaurant Gordon Ramsay from 2012 to 2016. She became the first female British chef to hold and retain three Michelin stars. Smyth won the Chef of the Year award in 2013 and achieved a perfect score in the 2015 edition of the Good Food Guide. Smyth regularly appears on TV shows such as Masterchef and Saturday Kitchen. Smyth's first solo restaurant, Core, opened in London in 2017.
- Thomas Keller : Thomas Keller (born October 14, 1955) is an American chef, restaurateur, and cookbook writer. He and his landmark Napa Valley restaurant, The French Laundry in Yountville, California, have won multiple awards from the James Beard Foundation, notably the Best California Chef in 1996, and the Best Chef in America in 1997. In 2005, he was awarded the three star rating in the inaugural Michelin Guide for New York City for his restaurant Per Se, and in 2006, he was awarded three stars in the inaugural Michelin Guide to the San Francisco Bay Area for The French Laundry. He is the only American chef to have been awarded simultaneous three star Michelin ratings for two different restaurants. He currently holds seven Michelin stars total: three at Per Se, three at The French Laundry, and one at Bouchon.
- The French Laundry : The French Laundry is a French restaurant located in Yountville, California, in the Napa Valley. The chef and owner of the French Laundry is Thomas Keller.
- the Time Warner Center : Time Warner Center is a mixed use (office/commercial and residential) twin-tower building in New York City.
- Columbus Circle : Columbus Circle is a traffic circle and heavily trafficked intersection in the New York City borough of Manhattan, located at the intersection of Eighth Avenue, Broadway, Central Park South (West 59th Street), and Central Park West, at the southwest corner of Central Park.

- Adam D. Tihany : Adam D. Tihany (born Transylvania in 1948) is a hospitality designer based in New York. He founded multidisciplinary design firm Tihany Design in 1978, and is considered the originator of the title "restaurant designer". His firm has designed hotel and dining properties at many notable properties around the world. Tihany was named one of the greatest American interior architects by The New York Times in 2001.
- Central Park : Central Park is an urban park in Manhattan, New York City, U.S. state of New York.
- Relais & Chateaux : Relais & Châteaux is a global fellowship of individually owned and operated luxury hotels and restaurants.
- Masa Takayama : Masayoshi "Masa" Takayama (高山 雅氏 Takayama Masayoshi) (born 1 May 1954) is the chef and owner of Masa, a three-Michelin-starred Japanese and sushi restaurant in Manhattan, New York City. He is also owner of Bar Masa, with two locations: one adjacent to his New York City restaurant, and one in the Aria Resort & Casino on the Las Vegas Strip in Paradise, Nevada.
- hinoki wood : Hinoki is described in the Nihon Shiki, one of Japan's oldest books, as "a good tree for building palaces" and was widely used to construct imperial courts, government offices, imperial gardens, shrines, and temples.
- garner : to collect something, usually after much work or with difficulty
- Phaidon : Phaidon is a global publisher of books on art, architecture, photography, design, performing arts, decorative arts, fashion, film, travel, and contemporary culture, as well as cookbooks and children's books.
- David Chang : David Chang (Korean: Chang Seok-ho 장석호; born August 5, 1977) is an American restaurateur, author, and television personality. He is the founder of the Momofuku restaurant group, which includes Momofuku Noodle Bar, Momofuku Ssäm Bar, Má Pêche, Milk Bar and Momofuku Ko in New York City, Momofuku Seiōbo in Sydney, Australia, the Momofuku Toronto restaurants Momofuku Noodle Bar (TO), Nikai, Daishō and Shōtō, and Momofuku CCDC in Washington, DC. In 2009 Momofuku Ko was awarded two Michelin stars, which it has retained each year since.
- Julia Hasting : Julia Hasting (born 1970) is a German graphic designer. She is the

Creative Director of Phaidon Press, head of the design department. She is known for the many best-selling books she designed such as Andy Warhol Catalogue Raisonné, magnum, A Day at elBulli, and Bruce Nauman: the True Artist.

- David Gelb : David Gelb (born October 16, 1983) is an American film director who directed the critically acclaimed 2011 documentary Jiro Dreams of Sushi. In 2015, he directed The Lazarus Effect.. He is also the creator of the hit Netflix series "Chef's Table."

2. The World's 50 Best Restaurants by Restaurant Magazine

The World's 50 Best Restaurants is a list produced by the British magazine Restaurant, based on a poll of international chefs, restaurateurs, gourmands and restaurant critics. The top restaurants are often forerunners of molecular gastronomy. Most of the restaurants serve haute cuisine, which is characterized by the meticulous preparation and careful presentation of food.

The first place on the list has been dominated by elBulli and Noma. In 2002 and 2006–2009, elBulli was determined to be the world's best restaurant, winning more times than any other restaurant. In 2010, Noma received the first place award. It was maintained in 2011 and again in 2012. After defending its title for the third time, chef René Redzepi said that 1,204 customers were wait-listed for the evening, compared to 14 customers from two years before. However, in 2013 El Celler De Can Roca took over the first position and Noma regained it in 2014. Eleven Madison Park in New York City is the current top restaurant, the first American restaurant to top the list since Thomas Keller's The French Laundry in 2004 (See Table 9-2; Wikipedia, 2018).

Table 9-2 shows a list of World's Best restaurants by year ranked first, second, and third from 2002 to 2017. This section introduces 3 World's Best restaurants such as Eleven Madison Park, Osteria Francescana, and El Celler de Can Roca according to author's selection criteria.

Table 9-2 World's Best restaurants by year

World's Best Restaurant			
Year	**1st**	**2nd**	**3rd**
2002	elBulli	Gordon Ramsay	The French Laundry
2003	The French Laundry	elBulli	Le Louis XV
2004	The French Laundry	The Fat Duck	elBulli
2005	The Fat Duck	elBulli	The French Laundry
2006	elBulli	The Fat Duck	Pierre Gagnaire
2007	elBulli	The Fat Duck	Pierre Gagnaire
2008	elBulli	The Fat Duck	Pierre Gagnaire
2009	elBulli	The Fat Duck	Noma
2010	Noma	elBulli	The Fat Duck
2011	Noma	El Celler de Can Roca	Mugaritz
2012	Noma	El Celler de Can Roca	Mugaritz
2013	El Celler de Can Roca	Noma	Osteria Francescana
2014	Noma	El Celler de Can Roca	Osteria Francescana
2015	El Celler de Can Roca	Osteria Francescana	Noma
2016	Osteria Francescana	El Celler de Can Roca	Eleven Madison Park
2017	Eleven Madison Park	Osteria Francescana	El Celler de Can Roca

(Source :Retrieved Jan. 19, 2018 from https://en.wikipedia.org/wiki/The_World%27s_50_Best_Restaurants)

1) Eleven Madison Park

Eleven Madison Park is a contemporary American restaurant located at 11 Madison Avenue, at East 24th Street, in the Flatiron District of Manhattan, New York City. It ranked third in the S.Pellegrino World's 50 Best Restaurants in 2016, and won the award for best restaurant in the world in the 2017 poll.

The restaurant, designed by Bentel & Bentel, is located in the landmark Art Deco Metropolitan Life North Building, facing Madison Square. The restaurant originally opened in 1998 and was owned by restaurateur Danny Meyer. In 2006, Chef Daniel Humm and Will Guidara began working at Eleven Madison Park and in 2011 they purchased it from Meyer. Humm and Guidara also own and operate the NoMad restaurant in the NoMad Hotel, opened in 2012, and Made Nice, a counter-service restaurant in Manhattan. Their restaurants are under the Make It Nice group.

The restaurant offers guests one multi-course tasting menu inspired by the agricultural bounty of New York and its culinary traditions.

Their Eleven Madison Park Cookbook was published in 2011; Humm and Guidara have released additional cookbooks since then, including: 'I Love New York: Ingredients and Recipes, The NoMad Cookbook, and Eleven Madison Park: The Next Chapter.

Description : The full review of Eleven Madison Park
(Source : Retrieved 27 Jan 2018 from https://www.flickr.com/photos/djjewelz/4580706340)

2) Osteria Francescana

Osteria Francescana is a restaurant owned and run by chef Massimo Bottura in Modena, Italy. After attending law school, Massimo Bottura opened Osteria Francescana in 1995.

In 2016, it was rated as the world's best restaurant in the World's 50 Best Restaurants. It was the first Italian restaurant to earn the award. It was also second best in 2015 and third best in 2013 and 2014. The first two positions in 2014 were won by Noma and El Celler de Can Roca respectively.

Osteria Francescana is rated with three stars by the Michelin Guide and holds the first position on the Italian food guide l'Espresso-Ristoranti d'Italia with a score of 20/20.

Description : The full review of Osteria Francescana

(Source : Retrieved 27 Jan 2018 from http://www.connoisseurs.me/destinations/1/italy/hotels/576/modena-osteria-francescana)

3) El Celler de Can Roca

One of the world's great dining destinations? Undoubtedly. Twice ranked No.1 in the world, El Celler de Can Roca is located in the medieval city of Girona in Catalunya, northern Spain. A decade ago, the Roca family moved the restaurant just up the road from its original location to its current site—an airy, purpose-built contemporary space complete with a huge kitchen.

The family dynamic: The three brothers who own and run the restaurant are each global leaders in their respective fields—Joan as a chef, Josep as a sommelier and Jordi as a pâtissier—so their combined creativity is a force to behold. Their food is complex, incorporating cutting-edge techniques and multiple ingredients to create highly stylised plates, but dishes are also designed to evoke memories, emotions and the landscape of the region.

A word about the wine: Fortunate diners will be invited to visit Josep Roca's magical walk-in cellar, where his passion for various grapes and regions becomes evident. The wine list, and the fabled wine pairing, more than lives up to its reputation for variety, originality and, most of all, quality.

What's on the menu: There are two: the shorter Classics menu of around seven courses (plus snacks) features established favourites such as 'prawn marinated with rice vinegar' and Jordi's edible perfume desserts; the longer and ever-changing Feast offering comprises 14-plus courses. Highlights might include flower of onion with comté cheese, cuttlefish with sake lees and black rice sauce, and charcoal-grilled lamb consommé.

Rocas on tour: In recent years, the team has closed the restaurant during August to embark on annual tours to South America, Turkey, the US and Hong Kong in order to broaden their collective culinary experiences. Global influences are then fed back into dish development, which in part takes place at their new La Masia (I+R) research and innovation space immediately opposite the restaurant site (Theworlds50best, 2017).

Description : The front door of El Celler de Can Roca in Girona, Spain

(Source : Retrieved 27 Jan 2018 from https://commons.wikimedia.org/wiki/File:El_Celler_de_Can_Roca.jpg)

3. Chef's Choice Restaurants by Year

When Restaurant Magazine produce an annual list of what it considers to be the best 50 restaurants in the World every year, the Chef's Choice list is also produced which is based on votes from the fifty head chefs from the restaurants on the previous year's list (See Table 9-3; Wikipedia, 2018).

Table 9-3 shows a short list of Chef's Choice restaurants by year from 2004 to 2017. This section introduces 3 Chef's Choice restaurants such as Central Restaurante, Lima, Peru, D.O.M., São Paulo, Brazil, and Mugaritz, Errenteria, Gipuzkoa, Spain according to author's selection criteria.

Table 9-3 Chef's Choice restaurants by year

Year	Name of Restaurant
2004	Tetsuya's, Sydney, Australia
2005	elBulli, Roses, Catalonia, Spain
2006	Pierre Gagnaire, Paris, France
2007	The Fat Duck, Bray, Berkshire, England
2008	Mugaritz, Errenteria, Gipuzkoa, Spain
2009	Noma, Copenhagen, Denmark
2010	The Fat Duck, Bray, Berkshire, England
2011	Osteria Francescana, Modena, Italy
2012	Mugaritz, Errenteria, Gipuzkoa, Spain
2013	Alinea, Chicago, United States
2014	D.O.M., São Paulo, Brazil
2015	Eleven Madison Park, New York, United States
2016	El Celler de Can Roca, Girona, Spain
2017	Central Restaurante, Lima, Peru

(Source : Retrieved Jan. 19, 2018 from https://en.wikipedia.org/wiki/The_World%27s_50_Best_Restaurants)

1) Central Restaurante, Lima, Peru

Central Restaurante is a restaurant located in the Miraflores District, Lima, Peru. Central Restaurante is the flagship restaurant of Peruvian chef, Virgilio Martínez Véliz, and serves as his workshop in the investigation and integration of indigenous Peruvian ingredients into the restaurant's menu. The restaurant is known for its contemporary interpretation and presentation of Peruvian cuisine. GQ Latinoamérica calls Central Restaurante "the heart of his [Virgilio Martínez Véliz] gastronomic philosophy." In 2012, Central Restaurante was named Best Restaurant of Peru by the Peruvian dining guide, SUMMUM. In 2013, Central Restaurante entered as number 50 in The World's 50 Best Restaurants as awarded by the British magazine Restaurant, and in 2014 jumped 35 places receiving "Highest Climber" recognition and ranking as number 15 in the world. On August 21, 2014, Central Restaurante for the third consecutive year was awarded Best Restaurant of Peru by the Peruvian Dining Guide, SUMMUM, and additionally received awards for Best Contemporary Peruvian cuisine and Best Sommelier.

Central has been named the best restaurant in Latin America for 4 consecutive years (2014, 2015, 2016 and 2017), and the 4th ranked restaurant in the world in 2015 and 2016

The cuisine at Central Restaurante is Contemporary Peruvian, and founder Virgilio Martínez Véliz has attempted to redefine Peruvian cuisine by introducing little-known indigenous ingredients from Peru's coastal region, the Andes highlands, and the Amazon rainforest. Examples of such ingredients include kushuru (cushuro), an edible cyanobacteria harvested in high-altitude wetlands; arracacha, a root vegetable from the Andes; and arapaima, a freshwater fish found in the Amazon River. Chef and restaurant commentator Geeta Bansal describes the cuisine as "fresh, and contemporary with beautiful plates."

Description : Photograph of main entrance of Central Restaurante, located in the Miraflores District of Lima, Peru.

(Source : Retrieved 27 Jan 2018 from https://commons.wikimedia.org/wiki/File:Central_Restaurante_-_Lima,_Peru.JPG)

2) D.O.M., São Paulo, Brazil

D.O.M. is a Brazilian cuisine restaurant in São Paulo run by Brazilian chef Alex Atala. Known for the use of native Brazilian ingredients, D.O.M. has been considered the best restaurant in South America since 2006 by Restaurant magazine, and since 2006 included in the S.Pellegrino World's 50 Best Restaurants list. In May 2012 the restaurant reached 4th place in the prestigious list. In 2014 Atala and D.O.M. won the Chefs Choice award.

Atala researches the ingredients used in his restaurant and supervises production in various parts of Brazil. Some of these ingredients are: tucupi juice, pirarucu and piraíba fishes, the herb jambu, and the tapioca from manioc flour.

Description : Picture of the restaurant

(Source : Retrieved 27 Jan 2018 from https://trendland.com/d-o-m-restaurant-in-sao-paulo/)

3) Mugaritz, Errenteria, Gipuzkoa, Spain

Mugaritz is a well-known restaurant in Rentería, Guipúzcoa (Spain), which opened on March 1998 under the management of Chef Andoni Luis Aduriz. It is considered one of the world's best restaurants since 2006 according to Restaurant Magazine and has been recently been ranked fourth in this toplist.

The restaurant is recognized by the press as "the most important gastronomic phenomenon of the world in recent times". Both Mugaritz and Andoni Luis Aduriz frequently show up on pages of media like "Omnivore", "Le Figaro" in France, "Brutus", "Cuisine Kingdom" in Japan, "The Trade" and "Republic" in Latin America and the U.S. "Time" or "The Observer." Mugaritz earned his first Michelin star in 2000 and, five years later, in 2005, the Michelin Guide awarded him a second one. The restaurant has also the highest rating by the Repsol Guide, the Three "Soles" and a multitude of honors for his innovative and creative activity in gastronomy.

In January 2011, The New York Times released Top 10 Restaurants in the World Worth a Plane Ride (See Table 9-4; Williams, 2011).

Table 9-4 10 Restaurants Worth a Plane Ride

Here are 10 restaurants around the globe to keep an eye on in 2011, in alphabetical order:

1. Aponiente El Puerto De Santa María, Spain
2. Benu, San Francisco
3. Dinner By Heston Blumenthal, London
4. M. Wells, Long Island City, N.Y.
5. Mirazur, Menton, France
6. Momofuku, Sydney
7. Restaurant André, Singapore
8. Restaurant Garzon, Garrzon, Uruguay
9. Tickets, Barcelona, Spain
10. Willows Inn, Lummi Island, Washington

(Source : Williams, Gisela, "10 Restaurants Worth a Plane Ride,"JAN. 7, 2011, Retrieved Jan. 19, 2018 from http://www.nytimes.com/2011/01/09/travel/09restaurants.html)

Time Magazine announced the top ten restaurants in The World in 2014. Here's a quick look at the top ten list. (See Table 9-5; Abend, 2014)

Table 9-5 The top ten restaurants in The World in 2014

1. Noma, (Copenhagen, Denmark). Cost of a meal for two, without wine: $600.
2. Celler de Can Roca, Girona, Spain. Cost of a meal for two, without wine: $390-480.
3. Osteria Francescana, Modena, Italy. Cost of a meal for two, without wine: $360-525.
4. Eleven Madison Park, New York, USA. Cost of a meal for two, without wine: $450.
5. Dinner. London, England. Cost of a meal for two, without wine: $230.
6. Mugaritz, Errenteria, Spain. Cost of meal for two, without wine: $470.
7. D.O.M. Saõ Paulo, Brazil. Cost of meal for two, without wine: $400.
8. Arzak. San Sebastian, Spain. Cost of meal for two, without wine: $530.
9. Alinea, Chicago, Illinois. Cost of a meal for two, without wine: $420.
10. The Ledbury, London, England. Cost of a meal for two, without wine: $270.

(Source : Abend, Lisa, "These Are The 10 Best Restaurants in The World," May 10, 2014,Retrieved Jan. 19, 2018 from http://time.com/94414/best-restaurants-world/)

CNN Travel recently compiled a list of 14 places enticing global diners to new restaurants in 2018. Here are 14 additions to the culinary must-try list for those keen to get in first at the hottest tables around the world (See Table 9-6; Dwyer, 2018).

Table 9-6 14 hot new global restaurants for 2018

1. La Rambla, Hong Kong
2. The Lord Erroll, Nairobi
3. Benjarong, Manila
4. Voyages by Alain Ducasse, Macau
5. Cleo, New York
6. Publico, Singapore
7. China Tang, Las Vegas
8. Taihei, Phuket, Thailand
9. Sensus, Dubrovnik, Croatia
10. Jean-Georges at The Connaught, London
11. The Lighthouse at Four Seasons Resort Seychelles
12. Le Comptoir de Pierre Gagnaire, Capella Hotel, Shanghai
13. COMO Uma Canggu, Bali
14. Galvin Dubai, Dubai

(Source : Dwyer, Chris, "14 hot new global restaurants for 2018," Updated 12th January 2018, Retrieved Jan. 19, 2018 from http://edition.cnn.com/travel/article/hottest-new-global-restaurant-openings-2018/index.html)

Note

- gourmand : someone who enjoys good food and wine
- meticulous : very thorough and with careful attention to detail
- elBulli : elBulli (Catalan pronunciation: [əɫ 'βuʎi]) was a Michelin 3-star restaurant near the town of Roses, Catalonia, Spain, run by chef Ferran Adrià.
- Noma : Noma is a two-Michelin-star restaurant run by chef René Redzepi in Copenhagen, Denmark. The name is a portmanteau of the two Danish words "nordisk" (Nordic) and "mad" (food). Opened in 2003, the restaurant is known for its reinvention and interpretation of the Nordic Cuisine. In 2010, 2011, 2012 and 2014, it was ranked as the Best Restaurant in the World by Restaurant magazine.
- René Redzepi : René Redzepi (born 16 December 1977) is a Danish chef and co-owner of the two-Michelin star restaurant Noma in the Christianshavn neighborhood of Copenhagen, Denmark. His restaurant was voted the best restaurant in the world by Restaurant magazine's World's Best Restaurants in 2010, 2011, 2012 and 2014. Redzepi is noted for his work on the reinvention and refinement of a new Nordic cuisine and food that is characterized by inventiveness and clean flavours.
- S.Pellegrino : S.Pellegrino is an Italian beverage company specializing in natural mineral water.
- Bentel & Bentel : Since its founding in 1957, Bentel & Bentel, Architects/Planners AIA has acquired a reputation for superior contemporary design.
- Art Deco Metropolitan Life North Building : The Metropolitan Life North Building, now known as Eleven Madison, is a 30-story art deco skyscraper on Madison Square Park in Manhattan, New York City, at 11-25 Madison Avenue.
- Danny Meyer : Daniel "Danny" Meyer (born March 14, 1958) is a New York City restaurateur and the Chief Executive Officer of the Union Square Hospitality Group (USHG).
- Daniel Humm : Daniel Humm (born 1976 in Strengelbach, Switzerland) is a Swiss chef and restaurant owner; he is chef/co-owner of Eleven Madison Park and The NoMad in New York City, the former a recipient of three Michelin stars.

- Will Guidara : William "Will" Guidara (born November 25, 1979) is a restaurateur based in New York City. Along with chef Daniel Humm, Guidara is co-owner of the hospitality group Make It Nice, established in 2011, which owns and operates Eleven Madison Park, The NoMad, and The NoMad Bar.
- the Make It Nice group : It is a hospitality group whose co-owner are Chef Daniel Humm and Will Guidara, which was established in 2011, which owns and operates Eleven Madison Park, The NoMad, and The NoMad Bar.
- Massimo Bottura : Massimo Bottura (born 30 September 1962) is an Italian restaurateur and the chef patron of Osteria Francescana, a three-Michelin-star restaurant based in Modena, Italy.
- l'Espresso : L'Espresso is an Italian weekly news magazine. It is one of the two most prominent Italian weeklies; the other is Panorama.
- behold : to see or look at someone or something
- fabled : famous because of being extremely good, beautiful, or interesting
- sake lees : Sake kasu (酒粕) are the lees left over from sake production. They can be used as a pickling agent, the main ingredient of amazake, a cooking paste to add flavor to food and as a marinade.
- La Masia : La Masia de Can Planes, usually shortened to La Masia, (Catalan pronunciation: [ɫə mə'zi.ə], English: "The Farmhouse"), is often used to generically describe the Barcelona youth academy.
- Virgilio Martínez Véliz : Virgilio Martínez Véliz (born August 31, 1977) is a Peruvian chef and restaurateur. He is considered one of the new generation of Peruvian chefs promoting the spread of Peruvian cuisine. He is known for his use of applying modern cooking techniques to indigenous Peruvian ingredients. Marie Claire magazine calls him "the new star of Lima's gastro sky."
- GQ : GQ (formerly Gentlemen's Quarterly) is an international monthly men's magazine based in New York City and founded in 1931. The publication focuses on fashion, style, and culture for men, though articles on food, movies, fitness, sex, music, travel, sports, technology, and books are also featured.
- Alex Atala : Alex Atala (Milad Alexandre Mack Atala, born June 3, 1968 in São Paulo, Brazil), is a Brazilian chef who runs the restaurant D.O.M. (Latin abbreviation

of Deo optimo maximo) in São Paulo.

- Andoni Luis Aduriz : Andoni Luis Aduriz is undoubtedly one of the most influential chefs of our times. Throughout his career, he has prioritized both culinary evolution and an interdisciplinary approach. This has allowed him to cross the established borders, and become a rebel in the kitchen.
- the Repsol Guide : The Repsol Guide is the result of years of experience and dedication to the world of travel. Since its first edition in 1979 its main goal has been supporting Spanish tourism and gastronomy, with a focus on being the best travel companion to help tourists enjoy the diversity of our landscapes and flavours.

References

AAA, "AAA/CAA Five Diamond Restaurants January 27, 2017, Retrieved Jan. 19, 2018 from http://www.aaa.biz/Travel_Information/Diamonds/Awards/2017/January%202017%20-%20 5D%20Restaurants.pdf

Abend, Lisa, "These Are The 10 Best Restaurants in The World," May 10, 2014, Retrieved Jan. 19, 2018 from http://time.com/94414/best-restaurants-world/

Bauer, Michael, "Benu, chef-owner Corey Lee rise to 4-star level," December 26, 2012, Retrieved Jan. 19, 2018 from http://www.sfgate.com/restaurants/article/Benu-chef-owner-Corey-Lee-rise-to-4-star-level-3250727.php

Dwyer, Chris, "14 hot new global restaurants for 2018," Updated 12th January 2018, Retrieved Jan. 19, 2018 from http://edition.cnn.com/travel/article/hottest-new-global-restaurant-open ings-2018/index.html

JBF Editors, The 2017 James Beard Award Winners,May 01, 2017, Retrieved Jan.19, 2018 from https://www.jamesbeard.org/blog/the-2017-james-beard-award-winners

Williams, Gisela, "10 Restaurants Worth a Plane Ride,"JAN. 7, 2011, Retrieved Jan. 19, 2018 from http://www.nytimes.com/2011/01/09/travel/09restaurants.html

Retrieved Jan. 19, 2018 from https://en.wikipedia.org/wiki/Central_Restaurante

Retrieved Jan. 19, 2018 from https://en.wikipedia.org/wiki/D.O.M._(restaurant)

Retrieved Jan. 19, 2018 from https://en.wikipedia.org/wiki/Mugaritz

Retrieved Jan. 19, 2018 from https://en.wikipedia.org/wiki/The_World%27s_50_Best_Restaurants

Retrieved Jan. 19, 2018 from https://en.wikipedia.org/wiki/The_World%27s_50_Best_Restaurants

Retrieved Jan. 18, 2018 from https://en.wikipedia.org/wiki/Sukiyabashi_Jiro

Retrieved Jan. 18, 2018 from https://en.wikipedia.org/wiki/Eleven_Madison_Park

Retrieved Jan. 18, 2018 from https://en.wikipedia.org/wiki/Osteria_Francescana

Retrieved Jan. 19, 2018 from https://en.wikipedia.org/wiki/Benu

Retrieved Jan. 19, 2018 from https://en.wikipedia.org/wiki/Masa_(restaurant)

Retrieved Jan. 19, 2018 from https://www.thomaskeller.com/new-york-new-york/per-se/restaurant

Retrieved Jan. 20, 2018 from https://en.wikipedia.org/wiki/Le_Louis_XV_(restaurant)

Retrieved Jan. 19, 2018 fromhttps://en.wikipedia.org/wiki/List_of_Michelin_3-star_restaurants

Retrieved Jan. 13, 2018 from http://dictionary.cambridge.org/

Retrieved Jan. 13, 2018 from http://encarta.msn.com/

Retrieved Jan. 13, 2018 from http://www.merriam-webster.com/dictionary/

Retrieved Jan. 7, 2018 from http://dictionary.cambridge.org/

Chapter 10

The Great Chefs

Portrait of Marie Antoine Carême
(Source : Retrieved 26 Jan 2018 from http://elestimulo.com/bienmesabe/emplatarte-breve-historia-parte-1-historia-de-la-cocina/)

"A lot of chefs are traditional and do it very well. But the ones who are the most successful are the ones who change things. That is why someone like Heston Blumenthal is a genius."

- Wolfgang Puck(born July 8, 1949), an Austrian-born American celebrity chef, restaurateur, and occasional actor

1. The Great Chefs in Culinary History

1) Marie Antoine Carême

Marie Antoine Carême was born into a working class family in Paris in 1784. When he died in 1833, he was recognized as the greatest chef of his time, and his name was familiar to the rich and famous throughout Europe.

Carême's colleagues, and the public at large, first discovered his talents with the publication of Le Pâtissier royal parisien(The royal Parisian pastrycook and confectioner) in 1815. It was only the third French treatise devoted entirely to French pastry, following Le Pâtissier françcedil;ois (1653) and La Pâtisserie de santé (1790). Carême's approach to pastry was innovative in more than one way. Not only did he perfect and diversify the uses of now classic preparations, such as génoise and biscuit (sponge cakes) or cream puff pastry, but appears to be the first to give recipes for fromage bavarois (pastry cream lightened with whipped cream and stiffened with gelatin) and its elegant derivative, the Charlotte russe.

In addition to presenting a far greater number of preparations than his predecessors, Le Pâtissier royal parisien was also one of the first to include a profusion of engraved plates throughout. Until then, French cookbooks contained very few illustrations, and when they did, they were almost exclusively devoted to table settings, some of which, nevertheless, included instructions for building very elaborate centerpieces for dessert tables. Carême's engravings, on the other hand, were for finished dishes. To the modern eye, they look less like pictures of food than elaborate architectural constructions: temples, helmets, waterfalls, all made of cooked sugar, almond paste, nougatine, and so on, to serve not only as centerpieces, but also as presentation pedestals for his elaborate pâtés and desserts. For Carême, the way food was served was as important as the way it tasted. He criticizes the way his predecessors seasoned and served "mountains of food," and he even attacks the size and shape of the china they employed.

In his great work on cookery, L'art de la cuisine française au XIXe siècle (1847), Carême carries his love of extravagant decoration to new heights for savory dishes, as well, standing cutlets and poultry on end and presenting them in a circle, turban style, or sticking whole fish and roasts with a wide array of decorative skewers garnished with truffles, crayfish, and mushrooms. More important, he entirely revamps the art of cookery itself, arguing, among other things, for a cuisine based on "velvety" sauces, rather than the thin, watery sauces favored in the past and for developing a series of basic preparations (brown and white sauces, court-bouillons, forcemeats, etc.) that would become the building blocks of classic French cuisine upon which entire families of preparations could be constructed by combining them or changing the main ingredient or a flavoring.

Despite all of his modernism, Carême preferred the monumental service à la française—in which all the dishes of a given course were placed on the table at once—to the newly-introduced service à la russe,in which they were kept hot in the kitchen, then served sequentially from platters passed by waiters. "Certainly this method of serving is conducive to good eating," he wrote, "but our service à la française is more elegant and lavish." His influence on French cuisine was enormous, and succeeding generations of chefs continued in the paths he had traced. It was not until 1903, when Auguste Escoffier published his Guide Culinaire, that Carême's authority was finally challenged, but his name is revered to this day as a great master whose contributions irrevocably shaped the course of French cuisine (Encyclopedia, n.d.).

2) Auguste Escoffier

Auguste Escoffier, born on October 28th, 1846 in the small village of Villeneuve Loubet in Southern France, is best known as a culinary writer and French chef who revolutionized numerous French cooking techniques and ways that kitchens are effectively managed. His journey down the culinary works began at a young age of 13, when he became an apprentice under his uncle, an owner of a restaurant in Nice. Under his uncle, he showcased an amazing prowess for both cooking and effectively managing a kitchen so much that he was soon hired by the Hotel Bellevue.

His journey inevitably took him to work at many illustrious and well known restaurants scattered throughout Paris and London; however, soon after arriving in Paris in 1870, Escoffier was called in to serve in the military during the Franco-Prussian War; however, his culinary expertise still lived on as he worked as Chef de Cuisine during his service. His active military experience also gave him a great appreciation and knowledge regarding canned foods and canning techniques to preserve foods over extended periods of time. He would be the first person to analyze canning techniques in depth and ways to make them even more effective than they already were.

Upon return home from service, Escoffier continued to work in multiple restaurants, constantly sharpening his culinary skills and frequently rising in the ranks of the culinary world through his sheer mastery of exquisite yet simple cooking. During his time in Monte Carlo in 1884, however, he met Cesar Ritz, an owner of the Grand Hotel who appointed Escoffier to manage the kitchens. Together, the two were able to bring significant changes to the hotel industry, constantly improving and raising the bar on hospitality and quality service.

In 1890, the two were contacted to work at the Savoy Hotel in London; here, Escoffier crafted one of his most well renowned recipes, the Peach Melba, a delicious dessert of peaches, raspberries, and creamy decadent vanilla ice cream. The dessert was inspired by and in honor of Nellie Melba, an Austrian singer who was a guest at the hotel. Later on, Ritz opened up several hotels from the experiences, the most famous of which is the Carlton in London, which took on Escoffier as one of the head chefs and kitchen managers. The reason for Ritz detaching from the Savoy Hotel was rooted in a few disagreements with the Savoy Hotel hierarchy, but the decision was so successful that many high-end clientele were soon found to replace Savoy Hotel with Ritz new hotel establishments. And Escoffier's culinary skills was a huge factor for attracting the high end crowds.

Escoffier's achievements and reputableness didn't just end here. His ingenious and elegantly simplistic way of cooking drove mass attention to his culinary craft. While most chefs around him relied on wasteful displays using garnishes or an abundance of sauces and overwhelming numbers of courses, Escoffier focused on simplicity and offering delicious foods that were well targeted and satisfying. He also greatly improved the efficiency at which kitchens can operate, doing away with what used to be wasted time and resources, as well as getting rid of redundant work in the kitchen.

Though he had far reaching impacts on the culinary world, Escoffier also made it a personal mission to give to the world of philanthropy, often creating programs to assist the poor and hungry in obtaining proper meals. His influence went as far as to gain attention from the French Government, who offered Escoffier the distinction of Chevalier of the Legion d'Honneur.

In 1921, Escoffier ultimately retired with his wife, Delphine Daffis, and died in 1935 in Monte Carlo (Culinarycareer, n.d.).

Description : Photograph of Auguste Escoffier

(Source : Retrieved 26 Jan 2018 from https://commons.wikimedia.org/wiki/File:Auguste_Escoffier_01.jpg)

2. 100 Best Chefs 2018

The Le Chef list is compiled by asking two and three-starred Michelin chefs to name the five chefs they believe represent the best of the profession, create the most influential cuisine, and helm a must-visit restaurant (FDL, 2017).

Michel Troisgros, of the storied Maison Troisgros restaurant in southwest France, has been voted this year's top chef by his fellow Michelin-starred colleagues, in an international survey which was revealed in Monaco on Sunday. Staying in France, chef Yannick Alleno was named second on the list, while chef Joan Roca from Spain was named in third.

Six of the top 10 on the worlds best chefs list come from France, with heavyweights like Pierre Gagnaire, Pascal Barbot and Alain Ducasse all sitting in the top tier. Chef Enrico Crippa, from Italy, made his first appearance in the top 10 in seventh position. Surprisingly, Troisgros also made his first appearance in the top 10 with the spotlight at number one.

Previous lists have come under criticism for being largely biased in favour of French cuisine and French chefs. The 2017 list has 35 of the 100 chefs from France, for 2018 that number hit 41.

The list also shockingly overlooks Latin America with only one chef, Alex Atala, owning a restaurant from that part of the world. Out of 100 chefs, just five of those listed are female: Dominique Crenn, Anne-Sophie Pic, Elena Arzak, Nadia Santini and Carme Ruscalleda (See Table 10-1; AFP Relaxnews, 2017).

Table 10-1 Best Chefs in The World – Top 10

1. Michel Troisgros – Maison Troisgros Restaurant (Ouches, France)
2. Yannick Alleno - Alleno Paris (Paris, France)
3. Joan Roca – El Celler De Can Roca (Girona, Spain)
4. Arnaud Donckele – Residence De La Pinede (Saint Tropez, France)
5. Pierre Gagnaire – Restaurant Pierre Gagnaire (Paris, France)
6. Emmanuel Renaut – Flocons De Sel (Megève, France)
7. Enrico Crippa – Piazza Duomo (Alba, Italy)
8. Pascal Barbot – L'Astrance (Paris, France)
9. Seiji Yamamoto – Nihonryori Ryugin (Tokyo, Japan)
10. Alain Ducasse – Plaza Athénée (Paris, France)

(Source : AFP Relaxnews, "French chef leads top 100 chefs ranking,"November 28, 2017, Retrieved 19 Jan 2018 from http://lifestyle.inquirer.net/280384/french-chef-leads-top-100-chefs-ranking/)

Note

- the public at large : 일반사회, 대중
- treatise : a written work dealing formally and systematically with a subject
- derivative : something that has developed or been obtained from something else
- Charlotte russe : a charlotte made with sponge cake or ladyfingers and a whipped-cream or custard-gelatin filling
- profusion : a large quantity of something
- nougatine : a chocolate with a nougat center
- extravagant : extreme, unusual, or unreasonable
- revamp : to change or arrange something again, in order to improve it
- revere : to very much respect and admire someone or something
- irrevocable : 변경할 수 없는
- prowess : great skill or ability
- reputableness : the quality of being reputable
- the Legion d'Honneur : [프랑스의 최고 훈장] 레종 도뇌르
- helm : to direct or steer

3. The World's Richest Chefs in the World

The world's most famous and richest chefs are much more than just chefs, they are brands. They are represented by more than their delectable dinners. Most of these famous chefs have their own television shows, product lines and books. In fact, several of them no longer actually cook at a restaurants because they are too busy running chains of restaurants, filming television shows, penning cookbooks and appearing on talk shows.

The national average for an executive chef is $71,000 a year. That amount is nothing to sneeze at, but the big name chefs are raking in millions. Cooking shows are now among some of the most popular shows on TV. Shows like Cutthroat Kitchen, MasterChef, Cupcake Wars, Greg's Grocery Games and Top Chef are raking in the dough while making the chefs who appear on them big time celebrities.

In the past, chefs were people behind the scenes who worked in hot kitchens, but today many of them are in front of cameras watching others do the cooking. The world's top cooking shows have turned several chefs into well-known celebrities and their celebrity status has put them on the millionaires list (Shondell, 2015). Let's take a look at 10 of the richest chefs in the world. Below are the top ten richest chefs in the World (Onyemaechi, 2017).

1) Alan Wong—Net Worth $1.1 Billion

Alan Wong is known throughout the world for the Hawaii Regional Cuisine restaurant and several others in Hawaii. He was born in Tokyo and has his connection to Hawaii through his half Hawaiian father. He is a well-known chef and was the judge on the show Top Chef season one. He even holds the credit to have organized a Hawaiian luau at the American White House for President Obama as a part of the Congressional picnic. He has gained awards like the Chef of the Year in 2001 presented by Santé Magazine. Gourmet magazine also ranked his restaurant as the sixth top restaurant in America. Even earlier in 1996 he had gained the name of the James Beard best Chef in the Pacific Northwest.

Description : Photograph of Chef Alan Wong

(Source : Retrieved 26 Jan 2018 from http://hjcc.org/wp-content/uploads/2015/06/Chef-Alan-Wong.jpg)

2) Jamie Oliver—Net Worth $400 Million

Jamie Oliver is a seasoned chef and restaurateur, he is known for his extra activities. He appears in a popular cookery show, has his cookery books, and organizes vivid events. He has held training for aspiring young chefs, promotion of fresh and quick meals in the British Schools, and has had the Jamie effect rolling over the whole of UK. His Tv appearance with the Naked Chef TV show was a huge hit, and then his top restaurant Jamie's Italian also rakes in enough profit. He has now expanded his restaurants from 17 to 27 in number. There are also profits pooling in from advertising and his Holdings Company.

Description : Photograph of Jamie Oliver

(Source : Retrieved 26 Jan 2018 from https://commons.wikimedia.org/wiki/File:Jamie_Oliver_(cropped).jpg)

3) Gordon Ramsay—Net Worth $175 Million

Gordon Ramsay has his income source from his restaurants and television show, and he is always in the limelight because of his short-tempered nature. His top television programs are Ramsay's Kitchen Nightmares and Hell's Kitchen. One of his primary income sources is the three-star rated eatery in London which brings in approximately €80,000 as profit each month. But in recent times, Gordon Ramsay's Holdings Company fell into serious debts.

Description : Photograph of Gordon Ramsay

(Source : Retrieved 26 Jan 2018 from https://commons.wikimedia.org/wiki/File:Gordon_Ramsay.jpg)

4) Wolfgang Puck—Net Worth $75 million

Wolfgang Puck has his income source from his excellent culinary skills, acting and even business insight. He has the credit of being the official chef of Academy Awards. There are over twenty restaurants, cookbooks and TV shows that have made him a familiar name in the industry. He began cooking by learning from his mother, and his first interest was in making pastries. His first cookbook was released in 1981 and soon after he went on to open his first restaurant named Spago. It was ranked among the top restaurants in the US in 2014 and has held its place since then.

Description : Photograph of Wolfgang Puck

(Source : Retrieved 26 Jan 2018 from https://commons.wikimedia.org/wiki/File:Wolfgang_Puck_2012.jpg)

5) Rachael Ray—Net Worth $75 million

Rachel Ray is a house hold name, with a favorite TV show in her name. She is one of the most popular celebrity chefs. In spite of the Rachael Ray show, she is also the host of several other shows like $40 a Day, Rachael Ray Tasty Travel, 30 Minute Meals and also the magazine Every Day with Rachael Ray. She has won the Emmy Awards for her shows as the Best Outstanding Service Show and Best Outstanding Talk Show. Her list of cookbooks is endless with most of them being popular sellers.

Description : Rachael Ray posing next to her personalized decal in front of a double-decker bus.

(Source : Retrieved 26 Jan 2018 from https://en.wikipedia.org/wiki/File:Rachael_Ray_Ride_of_Fame_Decal.jpg)

6) Emeril Lagasse—Net Worth $50 million

Emeril, who was born in Massachusetts, worked in a bakery as a teenager before discovering his love for cooking. He graduated from culinary school and fame crept into his life after being the executive chef of Commander's Palace. His list of awards is numerous including the James Beard Award. "Emeril's" was the name of his first restaurant, and now he has several restaurants making millions in profit. He is even popular for his shows aired on Food Network and makes guest appearances on other channels and shows. He has also written several cookbooks. His company "Emeril Empire" also has a good turnover of about 150 million dollars every year.

Description : Photographed signing his cookbooks and interacting with fans during a book signing at the Fort Lewis, Wash., Post Exchange Oct. 12.

(Source : Retrieved 26 Jan 2018 from https://commons.wikimedia.org/wiki/File:Emeril_Lagasse_book_signing.jpg)

7) Julia Child—Net Worth $38 million

Julia Child is not just a top chef but is also a great author and television personality. She is considered to be one of the people who had brought in the taste of French cuisine to the Americans. She died in 2004 at the age of 91 and was extremely active by hosting over 15 culinary shows till 2000.

Description : circa 1965: American chef Julia Child stands in front of a countertop, holding a whisk and a ladle by a mixing bowl, possibly on the set of her television series, 'The French Chef'.

(Source : Retrieved 26 Jan 2018 from https://www.independent.ie/life/food-drink/food-news/20-of-julia-childs-inspirational-kitchen-quotes-30506118.html)

8) Giada De Laurentiis—Net Worth $15 million

Giada De Laurentiis would thank all her assets to her show on Food Network. Her mother was an actress, and she turned her interests to cooking and food. Due to her love for chocolates she wanted to become a pastry chef. She was working as a chef in LA, before she attained her first recognition from Food Network. She has a catering business named GDL Foods.

Description : Giada de Laurentiis on 22 September 2013 speaking about her new Recipe for Adventure children's cooking books on the National Mall during the 2013 National Book Festival. She spoke from 12:00-12:30pm in the Teens & Children Pavilion.

(Source : Retrieved 26 Jan 2018 from https://en.wikipedia.org/wiki/Giada_De_Laurentiis#/media/File:Giada_de_Laurentiis_22_Sep_2013_National_Book_Festival.jpg)

9) Buddy Valastro—Net Worth $8 million

Valastro's reality show—Cake Boss has been the reason for his biggest success, and it has worked its charm on his business Carlo's Bake Shop. He took over Carlo's Bakery, his family business at the age of 17. The success of the TV show has led him to open two new branches in New York and New Jersey. He has currently three shows on TLC—Cake Boss, Kitchen Boss, and Next Great Baker.

Description : Photograph of Buddy Valastro

(Source : Retrieved 26 Jan 2018 from https://commons.wikimedia.org/wiki/File:Buddy_Valastro_at_the_Jersey_City_Mayoral_Inauguration.jpg)

10) Bobby Flay—Net Worth $6 million

As most seasoned chefs, Bobby Flay has cookbooks, restaurants and TV shows bringing his profit. He had aspired to become a chef as a child, and even requested for an oven on his 8th birthday. At the age of 17, he dropped out from High School and started working in a restaurant in setting salads. His skill was recognized and was what got him a sponsor to French Culinary School. Currently, he is working with ten restaurants, some of his own and at others as executive chef. He is a member of the Culinary Hall of Fame.

Description : President Barack Obama and celebrity chef Bobby Flay grill steak, corn and barbeque chicken at the Kick Off Young Men's Barbeque on the South Lawn of the White House, June 19, 2009.

(Source : Retrieved 26 Jan 2018 from https://www.flickr.com/photos/obamawhitehouse/3683211363)

4. The Most Influential Chefs in the World

This section introduces 3 most Influential chefs in the World such as L. Timothy Ryan, Ferran Adrià, and Paul Bocuse according to author's selection criteria.

1) L. Timothy Ryan

Lawrence Timothy Ryan (born January 16, 1958) is the fifth and current president of the Culinary Institute of America (CIA). Ryan, a Certified Master Chef, graduated from the CIA in 1977 and joined the school's faculty in 1982, and later moved to administration before heading the education division. In 2001, he became the first CIA alumnus and faculty member to become president of the college, in 2001. Prior to returning to the CIA as a faculty member, he spent five years as a chef in different aspects of the culinary industry. Ryan has received numerous accolades throughout his career from the American Culinary Federation, James Beard Foundation, and various other organizations.

Description : Tim Ryan, CIA President.

(Source: Retrieved 26 Jan 2018 from https://commons.wikimedia.org/wiki/File:Tim_Ryan_CIA_02.jpg)

2) Ferran Adri

Ferran Adria Acosta was born on May 14th, 1962. He began his culinary career in 1980 at age 18, as a dishwasher at the Hotel Playafels in Castelldefels. For a year, the Chef de Cuisine at the hotel taught him how to prepare traditional Spanish cuisine. At 19, he was drafted into military service where he worked as a cook. In 1984, at the age of 22, Chef Adria joined the kitchen staff of El Bulli as a line cook. El Bulli opened in 1964 by Dr. Hans Schilling and his Czech wife Marketa, and was named for the French bulldogs they owned. The restaurant received its first Michelin star in 1976 under Great Chef Jean-Louis Neichel.

In 1987, Chef Jean-Louis left El Bulli to open his own restaurant in Barcelona (Neichel's) and Chef Ferran Adria was put in sole charge of the kitchen. In 1990, Chef Ferran gained his second star for the restaurant and in 1997, its third Michelin Star. In 1994, Chef and his partner Juli Soler, his partner in the restaurant, sold 20% of their business to Miquel Horta for 120 million pesetas. This was a turning point for El Bulli. The money was used to finance an expansion of the kitchen and it opened the door to new clients who helped spread the word about the creative experimentation happening at the time in Cala Montjoi.

The experimentation is often referred to as "molecular gastronomy", but Chef Ferran Adria defines his cooking as "deconstructivist". He defines the term as "taking a dish that is well known and transforming all its ingredients, or part of them, then modifying the dish's texture, form and/or its temperature.Deconstructed, such a dish will preserve its essence, but its appearance will be radically different from the original. His goal was to provide unexpected contrasts of flavor, temperature and texture. Nothing is what it seems. The idea was to provoke, surprise and delight the diner, which it accomplished. The customer didn't go to El Bulli to eat, but rather to have an experience. El Bulli was only open six months a year, from April thru September. The rest of the year is spent in their Barcelona laboratory dreaming up and creating tastes for the next season.

In 2001, Great Chefs arrived at El Bulli to tape Chef Ferran Adria preparing a banana, strawberry, lemon gelatin and coconut foam for their Great Chefs of the World series which was airing on the Discovery Channel. Chef also prepared cauliflower couscous; caramelized Quail eggs and consommé tagliatelle for some Great Chefs specials. El Bulli closed in 2011 and Chef Ferran Adria retired at age 49, but plans to reopen it as a museum and center for creativity.

Description : LeWeb Paris 2013 - Conferences

(Source : Retrieved 26 Jan 2018 from https://www.flickr.com/photos/leweb3/11315101065)

3) Paul Bocuse

Paul Bocuse (pronounced [pɔl bokyz]) (11 February 1926 – 20 January 2018) was a French chef based in Lyon who was known for the high quality of his restaurants and his innovative approaches to cuisine (Wikipedia, 2018).

Bocuse was dubbed the "pope" of French cuisine and gave birth to the idea of the celebrity chef after he helped shake up the food world in the 1970s. He was at the forefront of the Nouvelle Cuisine revolution, sweeping away the rich and heavy sauces of the past in favor of fresh ingredients and sleek aesthetics that favored good health (Dwnews, 2018).

"Monsieur Paul was France. The pope of gourmets has left us," tweeted Interior Minister Gerard Collomb, announcing the chef's passing. "He was one of the greatest figures of French gastronomy, the General Charles de Gaulle of cuisine," said French food critic Francois Simon, comparing him to France's wartime savior and dominant postwar leader.

Prime Minister Emmanuel Macron also paid homage to the great gastronome. "Chefs weep in their kitchens at the Elysée Palace and everywhere else in France. French cuisine will continue to make him proud."

Bocuse was born in 1926 to a family of cooks dating back to 1765. He began his apprenticeship at the age of 16 and came to symbolize a certain type of French epicurean—a lover of fine wine, food and women.

The heart of his empire was L'Auberge de Collonges au Mont D'Or, his father's village inn just north of Lyon. The bistro earned its third Michelin star in 1965, and never lost one. "Monsieur Paul," as he was known, was twice named "chef of the century," first by a Michelin rival guide, the Gault-Millau, in 1989 and then again in 2011 by The Culinary Institute of America.

His imposing physical stature, combined with a larger-than-life personality, matched his bold dreams and his sprawling accomplishments. He could have settled for being a renowned chef with a prized bistro, but he chose to extend his culinary skills into an array of food operations ranging from haute cuisine to fast food that spanned the world.

As for food preparation, Bocuse said that many things go into great cooking but that his favorite ingredient was butter. "(It's a) magical product," he said during a visit to the Culinary Institute of America. "Nothing replaces butter."

Description : Paul Bocuse, French chef

(Source : Retrieved 26 Jan 2018 from https://commons.wikimedia.org/wiki/File:Paul_Bocuse2.jpg)

Note

- delectable : very pleasant, especially to eat or drink
- Cutthroat Kitchen : Cutthroat Kitchen is a cooking show hosted by Alton Brown that premiered on the Food Network on August 11, 2013.
- MasterChef : MasterChef is an American competitive cooking reality show based on the original British series of the same name, open to amateur and home chefs.[
- Cupcake Wars : Cupcake Wars is an American reality competition series which premiered on December 27, 2009 on cable television network Food Network.
- Top Chef : Top Chef is an American reality competition television series which premiered on March 8, 2006, on Bravo.
- luau : feast
- Santé Magazine : 프랑스 잡지
- Gourmet magazine : Gourmet magazine was a monthly publication of Condé Nast and the first U.S. magazine devoted to food and wine.
- the James Beard best Chef : The James Beard Foundation Awards are annual awards presented by the James Beard Foundation for excellence in cuisine, culinary writing, and culinary education in the United States.
- Holdings Company : A corporation that limits its business to the ownership of stock in and the supervision of management of other corporations. 자산관리회사, 지주(持株)회사, 모(母)회사
- Ramsay's Kitchen Nightmares : Ramsay's Kitchen Nightmares is a television program featuring British celebrity chef Gordon Ramsay first broadcast on Channel 4 in 2004.
- Hell's Kitchen : Hell's Kitchen is an American reality television cooking competition (based on the British series of the same name) broadcast on Fox. It is hosted by celebrity chef Gordon Ramsay. Two teams of chefs compete for a job as head chef at a restaurant.
- turnover : the amount of business that a company does in a period of time
- Culinary Hall of Fame : Culinary Hall of Fame is an institution honoring chefs and institutions that have made major contributions to cuisine and food preparation.

- accolade : an honor given to someone for their work
- Cala Montjoi : It is a bay on Catalonia's Costa Brava.
- L'Auberge de Collonges au Mont D'Or : the restaurant of the famous chef Paul Bocuse.
- the Gault-Millau : Gault et Millau [go e mijo] is a French restaurant guide. It was founded by two restaurant critics, Henri Gault and Christian Millau in 1965.
- LeWeb : One of Europe's biggest and longest-running tech conferences, LeWeb Paris attracts speakers and attendees from more than 80 countries around the world. Co-founders Loic and Geraldine Le Meur are particularly good at attracting big Silicon Valley names to the three-day event, that is now more than ten years old. In 2012, LeWeb expanded to hold its first London conference.

References

AFP Relaxnews, "French chef leads top 100 chefs ranking," November 28, 2017,Retrieved 19 Jan 2018 from http://lifestyle.inquirer.net/280384/french-chef-leads-top-100-chefs-ranking/

Culinarycareer, "Auguste Escoffier," Retrieved January 23, 2018 from http://www.culinarycareer.net/a_escoffier/

Dwnews, Famous French chef Paul Bocuse dead at 91, Retrieved 23 Jan 2018 from http://www.dw.com/en/famous-french-chef-paul-bocuse-dead-at-91/a-42236779

Encyclopedia, "Carême, Marie Antoine." Retrieved January 23, 2018 from http://www.encyclopedia.com/food/encyclopedias-almanacs-transcripts-and-maps/careme-marie-antoine

FDL, "100 Best Chefs 2018: Michel Troisgros Voted #1 by his Peers," November 26, 2017, Retrieved 19 Jan 2018 from https://www.finedininglovers.com/blog/news-trends/best-chef-in-the-world-2018/

Greatchefs, "Ferran Adria (Retired) formerly of El Bulli – Roses, Girona, Spain," Retrieved 19 Jan 2018 from http://greatchefs.com/chef/ferran-adria/

Onyemaechi, Dumebi, "10 Richest Chefs In The World Unveiled," Nov 14, 2017, Retrieved 19 Jan 2018 from http://kabalala.com/2017/11/14/10-richest-chefs-in-the-world-unveiled/

Shondell, "Top 12 Richest Chefs In The World," 11.10, 2015, Retrieved 19 Jan2018 from https://www.therichest.com/rich-list/the-biggest/top-12-richest-chefs-in-the-world/

Retrieved 27 Jan 2018 from https://thenextweb.com/event/leweb/

Retrieved 21 Jan 2018 from https://en.wikipedia.org/wiki/L._Timothy_Ryan

Retrieved 25 Jan 2018 from https://en.wikipedia.org/wiki/Paul_Bocuse

Retrieved 21 Jan 2018 from https://en.wikipedia.org/wiki/L._Timothy_Ryan

Retrieved 19 Jan 2018 from https://en.wikipedia.org/wiki/Paul_Bocuse

Retrieved Jan. 23, 2018 from http://encarta.msn.com/

Retrieved Jan. 23, 2018 from http://www.macmillandictionary.com/dictionary/british

Retrieved Jan. 23, 2018 from http://www.merriam-webster.com/dictionary/

Retrieved Jan. 23, 2018 from http://dictionary.cambridge.org/

Chapter 11

Korean Cuisine in the World

(Source : Retrieved 26 Jan 2018 from https://en.wikipedia.org/wiki/Korea)

"The World Food Travel Association estimates that food and beverage expenses account for 15% to 35% of all tourism spending, depending on the affordability of the destination."

\- World Food Travel Association

"In a 2017 travel survey, AAA's research revealed that an estimated 22 million Americans expect to take a culinary-focused vacation in the next 12 months."

\- AAA(The American Automobile Association)

1. The Role of Food or Culinary Tourism in Tourism Industry

1) What is Culinary or Food Tourism?

World Food Travel Association defines culinary or food tourism as the pursuit of unique and memorable eating and drinking experiences, both near and far (World Food Travel Association, 2017). It is now considered a vital component of the tourism experience. Dining out is common among tourists and "food is believed to rank alongside climate, accommodation, and scenery" in importance to tourists (McKercher, 2008).

Description : Terrace cafe, Rue de Buci, Paris, France.

(Source : Retrieved 28 Jan 2018 from https://commons.wikimedia.org/wiki/File:Terrace_cafe,_Rue_de_Buci,_Paris_July_2010.jpg)

2) Who are Food Travelers?

Research from our 2016 Food Travel Monitor proves that 93% of travelers can now be considered food travelers. By "food travelers", we mean travelers who had participated in a food or beverage experience other than dining out, at some time in the past 12 months. They may have visited a cooking school, participated in a food tour, or gone shopping in a local grocery or gourmet store. These are the types of activities that food travelers engage in. We also go on tours at food or beverage factories, participate in wine/beer/spirits tastings, and of course, eat out in unique or memorable foodservice establishments. We'll visit a chocolatier, bakery or gelateria to sample what makes the area famous. Most importantly, food travelers are explorers. We love to get off the beaten path and find the new (or new for us), unique or undiscovered experiences.

3) Economic Impact

Estimating the economic impact of food & beverage tourism is at best, very difficult. First, we would need to find how many travelers there are to an area. Then we would need to interview them to find out how much they spend on food and drink while traveling. We could dig deeper and ask them what percentage of their expenditures are for sustenance vs. a unique food or beverage experience. We would also have to factor out expenditures by locals. And how would you account for a visitor's spending on gourmet souvenir items in a grocery store?

Over the years, through our own research, secondary research, interviews and conversations, we have constructed our own impression of the value of food tourism.

By our estimate, visitors spend approximately 25% of their travel budget on food and beverages. The figure can get as high as 35% in expensive destinations, and as low as 15% on more affordable destinations. Confirmed food lovers also spend a bit more than the average of 25% spent by travelers in general.

Most governments publish data on total visitor arrivals and expenditures. Take the estimated economic impact of visitors to your area and multiply it by 25%. That is your estimated economic impact of expenditures on the food and beverage sector.

4) Culinary/Food Tourism Benefits

Food Tourism may sound like a great idea, but what tangible, measurable benefits can your involvement with our industry bring to you? Here's our short list of what you and the various players in your area can realize as you become more engaged in a sustainable food and drink tourism strategy:

- More visitor arrivals
- More sales (rooms/airplane seats/restaurant meals/wine/beer/car rentals/etc.)
- More media coverage
- A new competitive advantage or unique selling proposition (i.e. unique food and drink)
- More tax revenue to government authorities
- Increased community awareness about tourism in general
- Increased community pride about, and awareness of, the area's food and drink resources

2. Significance of Korean Cuisine in Tourism Industry

1) Korean Wave sweeping the World

The Korean term for the phenomenon of the Korean Wave is Hanryu (Hangul: 한류), more commonly romanized as Hallyu. The term is made of two root words; han (韓) roughly means "Korean", while liu or ryu (流) means "flow" or "wave", referring to the diffusion of Korean culture.

The Korean Wave encompasses the global awareness of different aspects of South Korean culture including film and television (particularly "K-dramas"), K-pop, manhwa, the Korean language, and Korean cuisine. Some commentators also consider traditional Korean culture in its entirety to be part of the Korean Wave. American political scientist Joseph Nye interprets the Korean Wave as "the growing popularity of all things Korean, from fashion and film to music and cuisine."

Hallyu has given Korean tourism a shot in the arm and helped tremendously in repositioning the Korean country image globally. As the movies, music bands and the soap operas gained popularity, people from many countries have been flocking into Korea to experience the Korean culture first hand. KTO has been very active in offering package tours which includes a visit to the shooting locations, the various towns and resorts made famous in the movies and soap operas and so on.

In 2015, Korea earned USD 15.2 billion from tourism, attracting a total of 13.2 million tourists. With the international tourist numbers hitting 1.1 billion in 2014 and international tourist growth forecasted at an annualized rate of 3.3% to hit around

1.8 billion by 2030, the Korean government is planning to increase its tourism revenues to USD 10 billion a year. The side effect of this tourist boom has been an increased popularity of Korean cuisine. It has been gaining so much popularity that the Korean government is planning a "Visit Korea Years 2016 to 2018" project, connecting with the PyeongChang 2018 Winter Olympics (Roll, 2018).

Description : Korea-Jejudo-Dae Jang Geum(L), Kim Soo-hyun as King Lee-hwon at the press conference for "Moon Embracing the Sun", 2 January 2012(R)

(Source : Retrieved 28 Jan 2018 from https://commons.wikimedia.org/wiki/File:Korea-Jejudo-Dae_Jang_Geum-04.jpg https://id.wikipedia.org/wiki/Berkas:Kim_Soo-hyun_as_Lee-hwon_(Moon_Embracing_the_Sun)_03.jpg

2) Korean cuisine becoming major cultural appeal to international travelers

One of the main implicit factors that tourists consider in choosing the destination is food (Ardabili, F. S. et al., 2011). According to the Michelin guide, If an establishment can offer exceptional cuisine which is worth a special journey, then it will be awarded three stars. It means that if any establishment offers exceptional cuisine and is worth three Michelin stars, tourists may choose it as a special journey.

In other words it means that an establishment can be a tourist destination as an attraction and food can be a destination as an attraction as well.

An international conference on cuisine and tourism was held in November 2000, in Cyprus. It was acknowledged, in a majority of articles, the local meals play a leading role in impressing tourists and increase the attractions of a region (Skinner, 2000; Van Westering, 2000).

Food is a very important factor in choosing destination. A 2016 survey by the Korea Culture & Tourism Institute found that international tourists decide to visit Korea mainly for shopping (67.3%) and culinary experiences (44.5%) (See Table 11-1).

Table 11-1 Considerations for deciding to visit Korea

(multiple responses, Top 10, unit: %)

Division	2016	2015	2014	2013	2012
Shopping	67.3	67.8	72.3	61.0	66.0
Foods/Gourmet meal	44.5	42.8	41.1	41.3	44.3
Natural Landscape	43.2	44.8	49.5	39.0	32.1
Historical and Cultural Remains	25.6	27.6	25.2	17.7	21.5
Elegant Culture: Fashion and Trends	25.4	23.6	19.8	14.8	11.1
Distance	12.2	8.9	7.0	11.7	16.9
Reasonable Travel Expenses	10.1	9.3	9.4	10.3	11.5
Well-made Recreational facilities	9.8	7.9	6.4	4.2	4.2
Leisure Time Available for Travel	9.6	10.5	9.3	9.2	7.6
Entertainment/Amusement Facilities	8.5	10.0	9.3	9.8	8.1

(Source : 한국관광공사, "2016년 외래관광객 실태조사 보고서, "2017.2, Retrieved 24 Jan 2018 http://www.tour.go.kr/)

Foreign tourists during their stay in Korea enjoyed culinary experiences. Ministry of Culture, Sports, and Tourism/ Korea Culture & Tourism Institute conducted "International Visitor Survey" against foreign tourists departing from Korea after visit in 2016. The survey found that they mainly did the shopping (75.7%) and enjoyed culinary experiences (51.0%) (See Table 11-2), and they were satisfied with Korean food (taste and service quality) (86.6%) (See Table 11-3).

Table 11-2 Activities during Stay

(multiple responses, Top 10, unit: %)

Division	2016	2015	2014	2013	2012
Shopping	75.7	71.5	74.0	70.9	72.8
Food Tours	51.0	47.3	46.4	39.0	48.4
Enjoy Natural Iandscape	28.6	30.0	31.7	17.6	13.3
Visit to palaces and historic sites	25.0	26.2	27.2	16.2	14.2
Amusement/Entertainment(Nightlife)	15.2	11.9	9.2	9.6	8.4
Business Operations	11.4	12.9	14.3	16.6	16.5
Visit to Museums and/or Exhibitions	10.5	10.5	8.9	6.5	6.7
Theme Park	10.5	8.3	8.9	7.1	5.1
Leisure, Relaxation(Resort)	8.5	7.6	7.4	8.9	8.6
Watching cultural performances, folk events, or festivals	7.9	6.9	5.1	5.5	5.2

(Source : 한국관광공사, "2016년 외래관광객 실태조사 보고서," 2017.2, Retrieved 24 Jan 2018 http://www.tour.go.kr/)

Table 11-3 Itemized Evaluation on Traveling Korea

(unit: %)

Division	2016	2015	2014	2013	2012
Immigration	87.2	87.7	87.7	82.4	77.7
Public Transportation	87.3	87.5	86.9	82.3	78.9
Accommodation	89.8	90.1	88.6	83.1	81.6
Food	86.6	85.8	85.5	81.1	82.0
Shopping	88.2	87.0	86.6	81.8	81.0
Appeal of Tourist Spots	85.7	84.0	82.1	75.9	73.4
Tourist Information Services	80.8	79.2	75.9	69.3	69.0
Communication(Language)	68.1	65.8	62.4	55.4	57.7
Travel Expenses	77.2	71.7	73.9	70.8	72.0
Security(Safety)	92.5	90.9	90.0	87.2	86.2

(Source : 한국관광공사, "2016년 외래관광객 실태조사 보고서," 2017.2, Retrieved 24 Jan 2018 from http://www.tour.go.kr/)

The Korea Culture and Tourism Institute conducted a survey in 2014 about the food preference of foreign tourists. According to the result, tourists loved bibimbap the most at around 35%, followed by bulgogi at 33%. Samgyeopsal, grilled pork belly, took the third spot at 30%. The survey concluded that foreign tourists' favorite food differed according to their nationality. While Japanese visitors loved galbi or ribs, and Chinese preferred samgyeopsal, Westerners from European countries or the United States enjoyed bulgogi the most, the survey revealed (Yonhap News, 2015).

Description : Bibimbap, Bulgogi,, Samgyeopsal, Galbi

(Source : Retrieved 28 Jan 2018 from
https://commons.wikimedia.org/wiki/File:Bibimbap_(8111593238).jpg
https://en.wikipedia.org/wiki/Korean_cuisine#/media/File:Korean.cuisine-Bulgogi-01.jpg
https://en.wikipedia.org/wiki/Korean_cuisine#/media/File:Korean_barbeque-Samgyeopsal-06.jpg
https://commons.wikimedia.org/wiki/File:Galbi_with_bamboo_leaves.jpg

3. 5 Ways Korean Food is Symbolic of Yin and Yang Principles

Korean food is not only known to be a healthy but is also deeply rooted in Yin and Yang principles. This is even symbolic in the prominent red and blue taegeuk symbol that is present in the middle of the South Korean flag (asianinspirations, n.d.).

These forces are both opposing and complementary; together, they govern the universe. As it should ideally be balanced, the five elements should also be present and in balance with each other. The five elements of Yin and Yang are associated with organs in the body and with five essential flavors, sour, bitter, sweet, spicy, and salty.

There's more to Korean food than the quintessential Kimchi. Korean food culture believes that food and medicine originate from the same root, therefore, there is no better medicine than food. Yin and yang principles are thus ingrained in the daily lives of Koreans.

Description : Closeup of Bibimbap ingredients(L), the Yin-yang symbol or Taijitu (太極圖), with black representing yin and white representing yang(R)

(Source : Retrieved 28 Jan 2018 from
https://blog.hellofresh.com.au/bibimbap-is-our-new-favourite-healthy-dinner/
https://commons.wikimedia.org/wiki/File:Yin_yang.svg)

Here are 5 ways Korean food is symbolic of the Yin and Yang principle:

1) The rice that is eaten by the Koreans on a daily basis is believed to have all five element energies in it. Here's how: It is cooked with water, in a furnace (wood and fire). The rice is steamed in the metal pot and the rice itself contains the best earth energy. By eating steamed rice, Koreans believe they receive the five elements' energy in every meal. Amazing, isn't it?

2) Korean dishes incorporate all five cardinal colours (blue, red, yellow, white, and black), each corresponding to the five basic elements. This ensures overall nutritional balance in every meal.

3) The traditional Korean table is shaped round to represent the universe with four legs on the earth, while the spoon is the yin and chopsticks are the yang.

4) Kimchi is a perfect example of yin and yang food as it has both the 'cold' and 'hot' elements like cabbage and chilli peppers. Grilled meats, with their juices and their fat, are supposed to be paired with fresh greens and sharp, earthy Doenjang, or soybean paste.

5) Bibimbap represents a careful balance of colours and ingredients and anything with the concept of 'bibim' of 'mixed' at its core.

Note

- affordability : 적당한 가격으로 구입할 수 있는 것; 감당할 수 있는 비용
- AAA : The American Automobile Association (AAA - pronounced "Triple A") is a federation of motor clubs throughout North America. AAA is a non-profit member service organization with over 58 million members in the United States and Canada. AAA provides services to its members, including roadside assistance and others. Its national headquarters are in Heathrow, Florida.
- get off the beaten path : 잘 다져진 길을 벗어나다
- sustenance : food and drink
- confirmed : fixed in habit and unlikely to change
- media coverage : (특정 사건에 대한) 매스컴의 보도(량)
- in its/their entirety : 전부, 온전히 그대로, 완전한 형태로, 전체로서
- Korea Culture & Tourism Institute : 한국문화관광연구원
- Ministry of Culture, Sports, and Tourism : 문화체육관광부(文化體育觀光部)
- quintessential : perfect as an example of a type of person or thing
- ingrain : firmly fix or establish (a habit, belief, or attitude) in a person

4. The Philosophy of Korean Food

Upon first glance no one would fully understand the significant effect that Korean food has on its traditional culture, other than a person's need to satisfy their hunger. Korean food is becoming more widely known for its popular dishes of bulgogi, bibimbap, and kimchi; enough to satisfy anyone's appetite. But why exactly are they becoming so popular? This is mainly due to the huge health benefits that these dishes carry, along with their unique flavors and colors. However dig deeper into the philosophical side of food, and what is the connection? You first need to understand that the mind and body are both connected with each other. Koreans believe that they are so interconnected that they believe a sick body can harm the mind and a strong mind can make the body healthy. Therefore food is also a huge factor underlying a sick patient's health due to its nutritious value.

This explains the typical traditional dining layout of a Korean meal, with colourful and plentiful dishes spaced around a table. This ancient philosophy is therefore in line with todays '5 A DAY' campaign, which aids the prevention of geriatric diseases and cancer due to the variety of fruits and vegetables on offer.

Description : 5 A DAY Your Way logo

(Source : Retrieved 28 Jan 2018 from https://www.rbkc.gov.uk/subsites/citylivinglocallife/gogolborne/eathappy/5adayyourway.aspx

Digging deeper into philosophical meanings, Korean philosophy is deeply rooted in the Taoist concept of yin yang or 'Eum yang' in Korean. Korean food both interacts and opposes itself in terms of its flavors and also its complimentary colors.

1) Sour flavor and the element wood.

Liver and bile works as a response to sour/acidic food. Acidic and sour food is useful in helping to 'cleanse' the liver and is therefore helpful to those who may have fatigue or a weak excretion of bile-juice. Distinctively, citron tea, apple, sesame leaf, grapefruit, and oats contain these characteristics.

2) Bitter flavor and the element fire.

This is related to the heart and the small intestine in our body. Stress and weight loss can cause indigestion therefore bitter foods can be helpful; these foods can be barley, lettuce, coffee and melon.

3) Salty flavor and the element water.

The kidney and the bladder are related to these forces. Salty food can influence these bodily functions and other related organs. Dehydration is an example of how salt and water interact, this characteristic can be controlled properly using salt, seaweed, bean, salted sea food, corn silk and watermelon are examples.

4) Spicy flavor and the element metal.

The lung and colon are affected by these interactions. Phlegm and bad coughs can be relieved by this flavor, as well as being helpful for sufferers of constipation and diarrhoea. Red pepper, onion, adlay tea, brown rice and peach have the characteristics.

5) Sweet flavor and the element earth.

These interacts help to work on the stomach and the spleen. Sweet food is specifically linked to helping indigestion. Therefore Yam, persimmon, ginseng, and beef, are particularly good for these symptoms.

In order to sum up all of these philosophical meanings Han Bok-ryeo, the director of the Institute of Korean Royal Cuisine wrote about Korean food explaining that 'It is a great source of energy; going beyond physical strength. Food and medicine are grown from the same root, and therefore there is no better medicine than food. People also add that the principles of ying and yang plus the five elements explain how all things in nature grow on the basis of mutual interactions. The twin energies created the five elements of wood, fire, soil, metal and water, and the five cardinal colors of blue, red, yellow, white, and black, corresponding to the five basic elements. The colored ingredients are blended, thus producing foods that allow the body to efficiently absorb the nutrients and to stimulate the appetite through five essential tastes; salty, hot, sweet, bitter, and sour'.

Therefore, when tucking into delicious Korean cuisine never forget that it is not just as good as it tastes, but also just as good for your body and mind!

5. Michelin starred-Korean Restaurants in the World

In 2015, U.S. households spent an average of $7,023 (12.5 percent of income) on food. Spending data on food is broken into two main categories: food at home, which includes unprepared foods like those bought at grocery stores; and food away from home, such as food at a restaurant. For the average household, spending on food at home accounted for about 57 percent ($4,015) of all food spending, while food away from home accounted for the other 43 percent ($3,008). Compared to lower income households, higher income households spent more money on food; higher income households also spent a greater share of their food budget on food away from home (See Table 11-4; Bls, 2015).

Table 11-4 How much americans spend on food annually

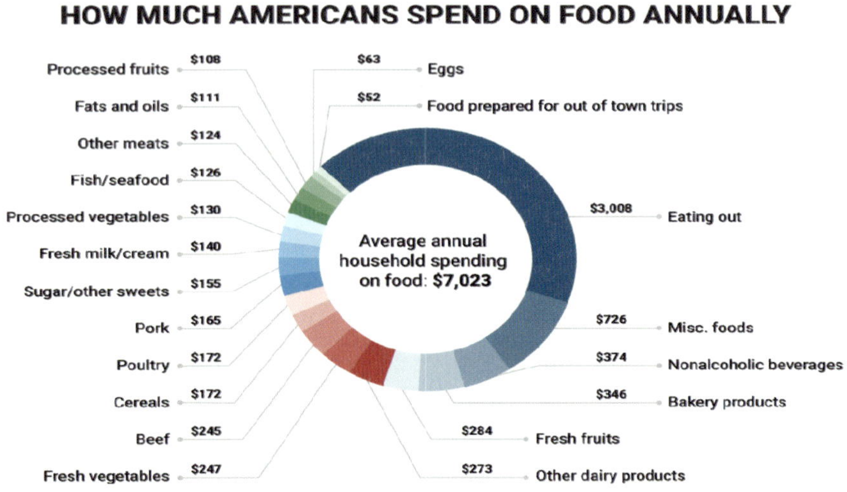

(Source : Morrell, Alex and Skye Gould, "A close look at Americans' food budget shows an obvious place to save money," Feb. 17, 2017, Retrieved 25 Jan 2018 http://www.businessinsider.com/americans-spending-food-bls-2017-2)

Table 11-5 shows that food away from home's share of total food expenditures rose to 50.1 percent in 2014, surpassing at-home food sales for the first time in 2014 (Economic Research Service, n.d.).

Table 11-5 U.S. food-away-from-home sales topped food-at-home sales in 2014

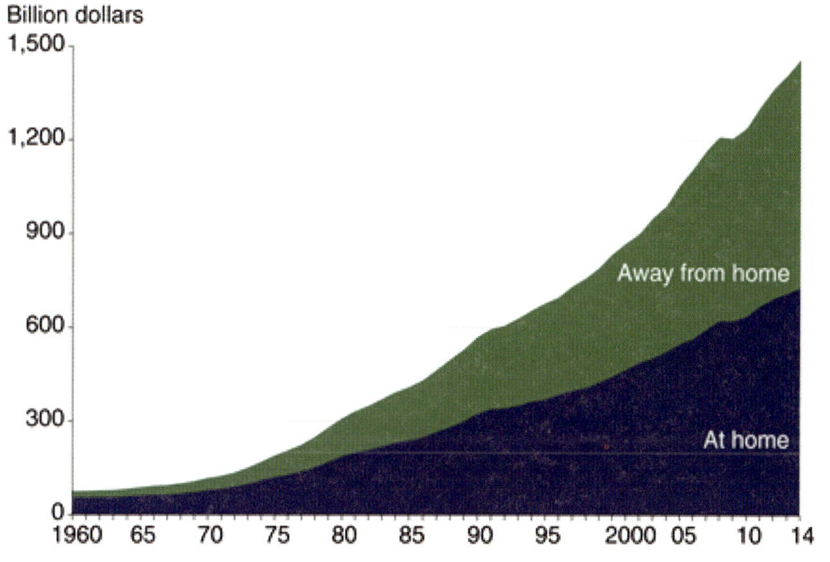

(Source : Economic Research Service, "United States Department of Agriculture, Food Prices and Spending," Retrieved 25 Jan 2018 https://www.ers.usda.gov/data-products/ag-and-food-statistics-charting-the-essentials/food-prices-and-spending/)

We do need to eat every day. Especially people, who leave their home for travelling, have to eat out of home. Restaurants serve a significant and vital role in tourism. Not only they provide tourists with food, but also they create their experiences. In fact, restaurants are not merely designed for eating purpose, and trying new local cuisines at a fine restaurant is one of the highlights of a trip.

According to a survey by Korean Food Foundation in 2016 the number of Koreanrestaurants in all markets outside Korea was nearly 31,511 in 118 countries. China had the largest number of Korean restaurants with 15,593 establishments, followed by Japan with 6,364. The United States came in third with 5,321 restaurants (See Table 11-6; 한식재단, 2017).

Below are Jungsik in New York, awarded with awarded with a Michelin star in 2013, and two Michelin stars since 2014, Yunke(尹家) in Tokyo, awarded two Michelin stars for 4 consecutive years from 2016 to 2018, and Hoba(ほうば) in Osaka, awarded with a Michelin star in 2013, and two Michelin stars since 2016.

Table 11-6 한식당 수가 가장 많은 국가 TOP 10

• 중국, 일본, 미국에 세계 한식당의 87%가 집중되어 있음(87% = 27,278/31,511)

순위	국가명	한식당 수	순위	국가명	한식당 수
1	중국	15,593	6	베트남	475
2	일본	6,364	7	말레이시아	316
3	미국	5,321	8	필리핀	267
4	대만	630	9	호주	250
5	캐나다	558	10	태국	213

(Source : 한식재단, "2016 글로벌 한식당 현황 조사 보고서," 2017.04, Retrieved 25 Jan 2018 http://hansik.or.kr/

1) Jungsik New York: Michelin 2-star restaurant

Cool, chic, and completely urbane, Jungsik is the epitome of contemporary elegance. Inside the large, neatly partitioned space, find rich browns and ivory furnishings with flattering lighting that is just bright enough to see your food clearly. The chairs are deep and tables are well spaced, but request a plush corner banquette for maximum comfort. Even the place settings show sculptural beauty through dark pottery and white porcelain. The ambience is fairly quiet and somewhat reflective. The modern cuisine is confident, complex, and happens to be leaning much more toward Europe than Korea of late. No matter—the cooking remains profoundly enjoyable. At the same time, the most inspired dishes are the ones that retain their heritage, as in the dome of seaweed-seasoned rice with cubes of smoked and torched yellowtail, finished with slivered lettuce. Before the red snapper arrives at the table, hot oil is poured overtop to cook the fish but also to yield incredibly crisped skin; then it is served with a brunoise of hearty greens and potatoes and rich perilla vinaigrette. Artful desserts include black raspberry and coconut sorbet with crumbles of spinach cake, yuzu meringue, and perfect berry slices.

Description : Inside view of Jungsik in New York

(Source : Retrieved 28 Jan 2018 from https://www.viamichelin.com/web/Restaurant/New_York-10013-Jungsik-360775-41102)

2) Yunke(尹家): Michelin 2-star restaurant in Tokyo

The female chef is a descendant of the Yun family, who were in charge of meal management for the king of Korea during the Joseon period. Using quality Japanese ingredients, she serves palace cuisine with no additives to preserve the yakuzen properties. The specialities are hairy crab ganjang gejang and black awabi yakuzen soup. They also pride themselves in their full-flavored, matured kimchi. This stylish restaurant has private rooms only.

Description : Front door of the restaurant

(Source : Retrieved 28 Jan 2018 from https://www.tripadvisor.co.kr/Restaurant_Review-g1066444-d7331239-Reviews-Yunke-Chuo_Tokyo_Tokyo_Prefecture_Kanto.html)

3) Hoba(ほうば): Michelin 2-star restaurant in Osaka

Food preparation is shared between the owner-chef, who studied Italian cuisine, and his mother who is in charge of the colorful namul and seasonal jijim. Risotto technique is used in the summer awabi and rice gruel. At the end come dishes like chilli pepper seasoned fish nitsuke or bone-in galbi. There are two time slots per day. This chic restaurant, located in Kitashinchi, is popular so be sure to book early.

Description : Inside view of Hoba(ほうば)

(Source : Retrieved 28 Jan 2018 from https://foodion.net/interview/araimasahiko?lang=en)

6. Five of the Best Korean Restaurants around the World

The World's 50 Best Restaurants is hosting its first Korean Dinners series this June in association with La Main magazine, bringing five of Seoul's top chefs to cook with two of the finest cooks in New York (Price, 2016)

In the spirit of sharing great Korean cuisine with the world, we asked our Academy Chairs—the experts in global gastronomy—for their Korean restaurant recommendations, from fine dining to casual-but-authentic local spots. Here's what they came up with:

1) Sky Kong Kong, Bristol, England

Recommended by: Xanthe Clay, 50 Best Academy Chair for UK and Ireland

Expert tip: "Located in a former pie shop by an inner city underpass, Sky Kong Kong has just one refectory table and one chef. Hwi Shim, known as Wizzy, serves up a meal of heart-warming Korean home cooking—there's no menu; the food just comes—for £12.50 a head. Dinner might feature grilled sea bream, braised pork with homemade miso and chicken in ginseng broth while many of the vegetables, including sesame leaves for pickling, come from her allotment. Bring your own drinks or try green tea or ginseng juice."

Description : Exterior view of Sky Kong Kong

(Source : Retrieved 28 Jan 2018 from https://wayoutwestfood.wordpress.com/)

2) Mandoobar, Paris, France

Recommended by: Nicolas Chatenier, 50 Best Academy Chair for France

Expert tip: "Mandoobar a counter-style restaurant specialized in mandoos, which are Korean raviolis. This place is refined and highly rated by local French guides."

Description : Inside view of Mandoobar

(Source : Retrieved 28 Jan 2018 from http://www.carnetsduneflaneuse.fr/les-tapas-coreens-du-mandoobar/)

3) Gogi, Chicago, USA

Recommended by: Steve Dolinsky, 50 Best Academy Chair for mid USA and mid Canada

Expert tip: "The barbecue at Gogi is fantastic—well-marbled and marinated kalbi, and always grilled over live fire and charcoals. Especially good are the haemul pajeon (seafood pancake) served crispier than most, and a phenomenal kimchi fried rice with pork belly that is among my favourite late-night snacks."

Description : Inside view of Gogi

(Source : Retrieved 28 Jan 2018 from https://www.chicagoreader.com/chicago/mike-sula-reviews-gogi-korean-barbecue-west-ridge/Content?oid=11328261)

4) Handung, Tokyo, Japan

Recommended by: Takanori Nakamura, 50 Best Academy Chair for Japan

Expert tip: "As well as the high quality of the yakiniku ingredients, such as various meat and vegetables, the kimchi made by chef Ms. Kim is fantastic and a must-try dish. Even Koreans are impressed and surprised by this restaurant—I've had people tell me they haven't had such delicious kimchi even in Korea. This really is a place to experience authentic Korean cuisine."

Description : Inside view of Handung and Kimchi

(Source : Retrieved 28 Jan 2018 from http://www.jnto.go.jp/restaurant-search/eng/detail.php?rst_code=a525200)

5) Moon Park, Sydney, Australia

Recommended by: Pat Nourse, 50 Best Academy Chair for Oceania, Australia & New Zealand

Expert tip: "Moon Park is that perfect modern Korean restaurant: deeply invested in the culture of Korea, yet very much a product of its Sydney environment, offering grower Champagnes and natural wines from around the world alongside soju and OB lager. The ssäm of smoked eel and puffed rice on a nasturtium leaf is an absolute must."

Description : Inside view of Moon Park and Kimchi at Moon Park

(Source : Retrieved 28 Jan 2018 from http://www.un-fold-ed.com/2015/02/01/moon-park-sydney/)

7. Promoting Korean Cuisine around the World

Korea has supported for Korean food promotion in terms of financial support since May 2009, when the Hansik Globalization Development Agency was inaugurated, which is comprised of 36 members from relevant government departments, academic institutions and CEOs from the food industry. The government-funded Hansik Foundation was established in March 2010, and in March 2011 the Foodservice Industry Promotion Act was enacted. These initiatives are set to ensure that the Hansik Globalization Project is well-equipped to become a driving force (Choi, 2012).

The international image of Korean cuisine is still not as strong as that of Japanese or Chinese cuisine. To promote culinary tourism in Korea and improve the international image of Korean cuisine, the Korea Tourism Organization has a comprehensive introduction to Korean cuisine, using detailed written descriptions and photos on its website. Let's take a look at it!

The website includes "Introduction" (including "General Kinds of Korean food," "Ingredients of Korean Food," and "Food Story"), "What to Eat" (including "Kimchi," "Bibimbap," "Royal Cuisine," "Traditional Liquors & Wines," and "Popular Snacks"), "Where to Eat" (e.g. "Restaurant Search," "Gourmet Tour Course," "Food-Themed Destinations in Korea," and "Special Diets), "How to Cook" (e.g. "Easy Korean Cooking," "Learning the Basics," and "Recipes"), and "Recommended Food (including "Michelin Guide Seoul," and Recommended Food Columns). This website thus offers an in-depth guide to Korean cuisine for those interested in Korean cuisine and traditional Korean food culture (English.visitkorea, 2018).

Note

- Upon first glance (=At first glance) : upon first seeing or considering something
- other than : …외에
- 5 A DAY : 5 A Day is any of various national campaigns in countries such as the United States, the United Kingdom, France, and Germany, to encourage the consumption of at least five portions of fruit and vegetables each day, following a recommendation by the World Health Organization that individuals consume "a minimum of 400g of fruit and vegetables per day (excluding potatoes and other starchy tubers).
- geriatric : relating to old age, or to the process of getting older
- bile : 담즙
- kidney : 신장, 콩팥
- bladder : 방광
- colon : 결장(結腸)
- phlegm : 가래, 담
- constipation : 변비
- diarrhoea : 설사
- adlay tea : 율무 차
- spleen : 지라, 비장
- the Institute of Korean Royal Cuisine : 궁중음식연구원
- tuck into : to eat food with enthusiasm because you like it or because you are hungry
- Korean Food Foundation : 한식재단
- chic : fashionable and attractive in style
- epitome : a typical or ideal example
- no matter : It doesn't matter; it's not important.
- brunoise : finely diced vegetables that are cooked in butter and used to flavor soups and sauces
- vinaigrette : a sauce for salads and cold vegetables, made from oil, vinegar, and spices
- meringue : a sweet food made from a mixture of sugar and egg whites
- yakuzen : "Yakuzen" is a form of medicinal cooking based on the theories of Oriental medicine. 약선(한방)

- awabi : sushi made from abalone
- gruel : a food made by boiling crushed grain in water or milk, often eaten by poor people in the past
- fish nitsuke (につけ; 煮付け) : 생선조림
- slot : an amount of time that is officially allowed for a single event in a planned order of activities or events
- La Main magazine : 라망매거진(la main)에서 la main은 불어로 '손'이라는 뜻이다. 셰프, 스타일리스트, 포토그래퍼, 에디터, 그리고 디자이너 등이 만든 쿠킹 전문 매거진이다. (See https://lamainmagazinekr.modoo.at/)
- Xanthe Clay : 영국 텔레그래프지 음식 칼럼니스트인 산시 클레이
- refectory : a dining hall (as in a monastery or college)
- allotment : the act of distributing by allotting or apportioning; distribution according to a plan
- ravioli : pasta in the form of little cases of dough containing a savory filling (as of meat or cheese)
- phenomenal : extremely impressive or surprising
- yakiniku : Yakiniku (焼き肉 or 焼肉), meaning "grilled meat", is a Japanese term that, in its broadest sense, refers to grilled meat cuisine.
- Pat Nourse : Pat Nourse (born 1977) is an Australian restaurant critic and food writer. He is currently employed by Australian Gourmet Traveller magazine as their chief restaurant critic and deputy editor. He also writes about Australia for the American food magazine Gourmet, and is the Australian member of the voting academy for the World's 50 Best Restaurants. He has been a contributor to The Age Good Food Guide and The Sydney Morning Herald Good Food Guide, among other publications.
- grower Champagnes : Grower Champagnes are sparkling wines made in the Champagne region of France that are produced by the same estate that owns the vineyards from which the grapes come.
- nasturtium leaf : 한련(원예 식물의 하나. 샐러드에 넣어 먹기도 함)
- The Hansik Globalization Development Agency : 한식세계화추진단
- Hansik Foundation : 한식재단
- The Foodservice Industry Promotion Act : 외식산업진흥법
- The Korea Tourism Organization : 한국관광공사

References

Ardabili, F. S. et al. (2011), "The Role of Food and Culinary Condition in Tourism Industry", Middle- East Journal of Scientific Research, vol. 9, no.6, pp. 826-833.

Asianinspirations, "5 Ways Korean Food is Symbolic of Yin and Yang Principles," Retrieved 22 Jan 2018 from https://asianinspirations.com.au/asian-culture/5-ways-korean-food-is-symbolic-of-yin-and-yang-principles/

Bureau of Labor Statistics, U.S. Department of Labor, "The Economics Daily,High-income households spent half of their food budget on food away fromhome in 2015," October 05, 2016, Retrieved 25 Jan 2018 from https://www.bls.gov/opub/ted/2016/high-income-households-spent-half-of-their-food-budget-on-food-away-from-home-in-2015.htm

Choi, Jong-Moon, (2012) Chapter 8 Globalising Korean food and stimulating inboundtourism, FOOD AND THE TOURISM EXPERIENCE: THE OECD-KOREA WORKSHOP: 126.

Economic Research Service, "United States Department of Agriculture, Food Pricesand Spending," Retrieved 25 Jan 2018 https://www.ers.usda.gov/data-products/ag-and-food-statistics-charting-the-essentials/food-prices-and-spending/)

Laura, "The Philosophy of Korean Food," July 15, 2013, Retrieved 22 Jan 2018 from https://asiacrunchdotcom1.wordpress.com/2013/07/15/the-philosophy-of-korean-food/

McKercher, Bob; Okumus, Fevzi; Okumus, Bendegul (2008). "Food Tourism as a Viable Market Segment: It's All How You Cook the Numbers!". Journal of Travel& Tourism Marketing. 25 (2): 137-148.

MICHELIN guide inspectors, "MICHELIN Guide's Point Of View," Retrieved 22 Jan 2018 from https://guide.michelin.com/us/new-york/jungsik/restaurant

MICHELIN guide inspectors, Retrieved 22 Jan 2018 from http://gm.gnavi.co.jp/shop/0115036302/

MICHELIN guide inspectors, Retrieved 22 Jan 2018 from http://gm.gnavi.co.jp/shop/0515032901/

Morrell, Alex and Skye Gould, "A close look at Americans' food budget shows an obvious place to save money," Feb. 17, 2017, Retrieved 25 Jan 2018 http://www.businessinsider.com/americans-spending-food-bls-2017-2)

Price, Laura, Five of the best Korean restaurants around the world, 22/04/2016, https://www.the

worlds50best.com/blog/News/five-of-the-best-korean-restaurants-around-the-world.html

Roll, Martin, "Korean Wave (Hallyu) – The Rise of Korea's Cultural Economy & PopCulture," Jan 2018, Retrieved 22 Jan 2018 from https://martinroll.com/resources/articles/asia/korean-wave-hallyu-the-rise-of-koreas-cultural-economy-pop-culture/

Skinner, P., 2000. Quality Food/Wine Tourism: Compatibility with Local Culinary Tradition. Paper Presented at the Local Food and Tourism InternationalConference, Larnaka, Cyprus. Madrid: World Tourism Organization.

Van Westering, J., Y. Poria and N. Liapis, 2000. Using Food and Food History as aResource for Tourism. Paper Presented at the Local Food and TourismInternational Conference, Larnaka, Cyprus. Madrid: World Tourism Organization.

World Food Travel Association, "What is Food Tourism?" Retrieved 14 Jan2018 from https://www.worldfoodtravel.org/cpages/what-is-food-tourism

Yonhap News, "Foreign tourists grade Korean cuisine with a "C" rating," March 16th, 2015, Retrieved 25 Jan 2018 https://www.koreaboo.com/news/foreign-tourists-grade-korean-cuisine-c-rating/

한국관광공사, "2016년 외래관광객 실태조사 보고서,"2017.2, Retrieved 24 Jan 2018 http://www.tour.go.kr/

한식재단, "2016 글로벌 한식당 현황 조사 보고서," 2017.04, Retrieved 25 Jan 2018 http://hansik.or.kr/

Retrieved 26 Jan 2018 http://english.visitkorea.or.kr/enu/FOD/FO_ENG_1_4.jsp

Retrieved 25 Jan 2018 https://en.wikipedia.org/wiki/Korean_Wave

Retrieved 25 Jan 2018 from http://dictionary.cambridge.org/

Retrieved 25 Jan 2018 from http://encarta.msn.com/

Retrieved 25 Jan 2018 from http://www.merriam-webster.com/dictionary/

Retrieved 25 Jan 2018 from http://dictionary.cambridge.org/

Retrieved 28 Jan 2018 from http://www.visitkorea.or.kr/intro.html

편저자 : Kang, Kyung Jae

- 전북대학교 졸업(학사)
- 호원대학교 졸업(학사)
- 경기대학교 대학원 관광경영학과 졸업 (경영학 석사)
- 경기대학교 대학원 관광경영학과 졸업 (경영학 박사)
- 전 군산 미공군기지 제8헌병대대 언어전문관
- 전 경기대학교, 호원대학교, 남서울대학교, 혜전대학, 혜천대학, 군장공업대학, 원광보건대학 강사
- 전 혜전대학 호텔조리계열 학부장
- 전 혜전대학 호텔조리외식계열 계열장
- 전 혜전대학 호텔조리외식계열 음료경영전공 전공장
- 전 혜전대학 호텔조리외식계열 일식전공 전공장
- 전 혜전대학교 호텔조리외식계열 조리유학전공 전공장
- 전 혜전대학교 호텔조리외식계열 글로벌조리전공 전공장
- 전 혜전대학교 호텔조리외식계열 교수
- 현 혜전대학교 호텔조리과 교수
- 저서 : 신관광영어강독, 학문사(1998)
  Hotel & Food Service Cuisine English, 백산출판사(1999)
  Guide to the Student Chef, 대왕사(2001)
  Guide to Culinary English, 대왕사(2003)
  Guide to Food Styling English, 대왕사(2005)
  Guide to Recipe for the Student Chef, 대왕사(2006)
  Guide to Culinary and Foodservice English, LBH(2007)
  Guide to Kitchen English, 백산출판사(2008)
  Guide to Recipes of Oriental Cuisines, 대왕사(2009)
  Guide to the Culinary Industry, 백산출판사(2010)
  Guide to Culinary Readings(Ⅰ), 백산출판사(2012)
  Guide to Culinary Readings(Ⅱ), 백산출판사(2012)
  Guide to Culinary Readings(Ⅲ), 백산출판사(2013)
  Guide to Practical English for Japanese Cuisine, 가담플러스(2014)
  Guide to Practical English for Korean Cuisine, 백산출판사(2016)
- 논문 : 호텔 레스토랑의 데이터베이스 마케팅에 관한 연구 외 다수

저자와의
합의하에
인지첩부
생략

Guide to Understanding the Culinary Industry

2018년 2월 20일 초판 1쇄 인쇄
2018년 2월 25일 초판 1쇄 발행

편저자 Kang, Kyung Jae
펴낸이 진욱상
펴낸곳 (주)백산출판사
교　정 편집부
본문디자인 오행복
표지디자인 오정은

등　록 2017년 5월 29일 제406-2017-000058호
주　소 경기도 파주시 회동길 370(백산빌딩 3층)
전　화 02-914-1621(代)
팩　스 031-955-9911
이메일 edit@ibaeksan.kr
홈페이지 www.ibaeksan.kr

ISBN 979-11-88892-25-9
값 20,000원